REBREATHER

The Line, It's Width and the War Drone

ALR028

Published by

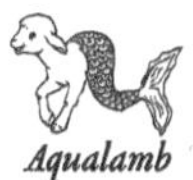

REBREATHER

Barley Rantilla - Vocals & Guitar
Steve Gardner - Drums
Steve Wishnewski - Vocals & Bass

RECORDING CREDITS

Engineered, Recorded and Mixed by Josh Roman at Mindrocket Recording Studio - West Middlesex, PA
Mastered by Carl Saff at Saff Mastering - Chicago, IL
"Drown" features Frayle: Gwyn Strang (Additional Vocals) and Sean Bilovecky (Additional Guitars)
"Silent H" features: Shy Kennedy (Additional Vocals)

IMAGE CREDITS

Eric Palmerlee: illustrations on pgs 2-38. David Slebodnik: Drown illustration on pgs 54-55. Jasmyn Iwanejko and Ryan Iwanejko: photos on pgs 56-65. Beth Gillam, Lisa Rouse, Jessica King: drone photos on pgs 66, 70. Thad Minnick: illustrations on pgs 70, 75. Thaddaeus Allen: illustrations on pgs 68-69, 76-77. Mollie Crowe (Little Blackbird): all other photography.

THANK YOU

Johnathan, Eric & everyone at Aqualamb Records. Josh Roman & Mindrocket Recording Studio. Carl Saff & all at Saff Mastering. The Offerdahl's & Our Westside Bowl family. Joe Sudrovek & Everyone at Gorilla Joe Printing. All the bands that let us share the stage. The Gerhart's & all at Noble Creature Cask House. Kathy, John & Everyone at The Grog Shop. Ben DeRolph & The Crew at Spacebar. The 3 F's: Friends, Family & Fans. Without you all, none of this would be possible

All songs written and performed by Rebreather.

First Printing: Edition of 500
ISBN: 979-8-9857365-3-3

aqualamb.org
rebreatherband.com

CONTENTS

SONGS

FEATURES

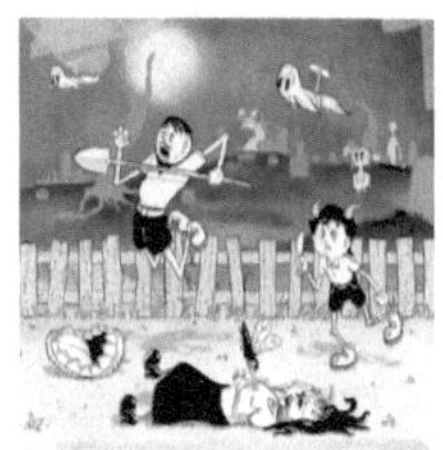

The music for *The Line, It's Width and the War Drone*
can be downloaded via the link below:

aqualamb.org/028

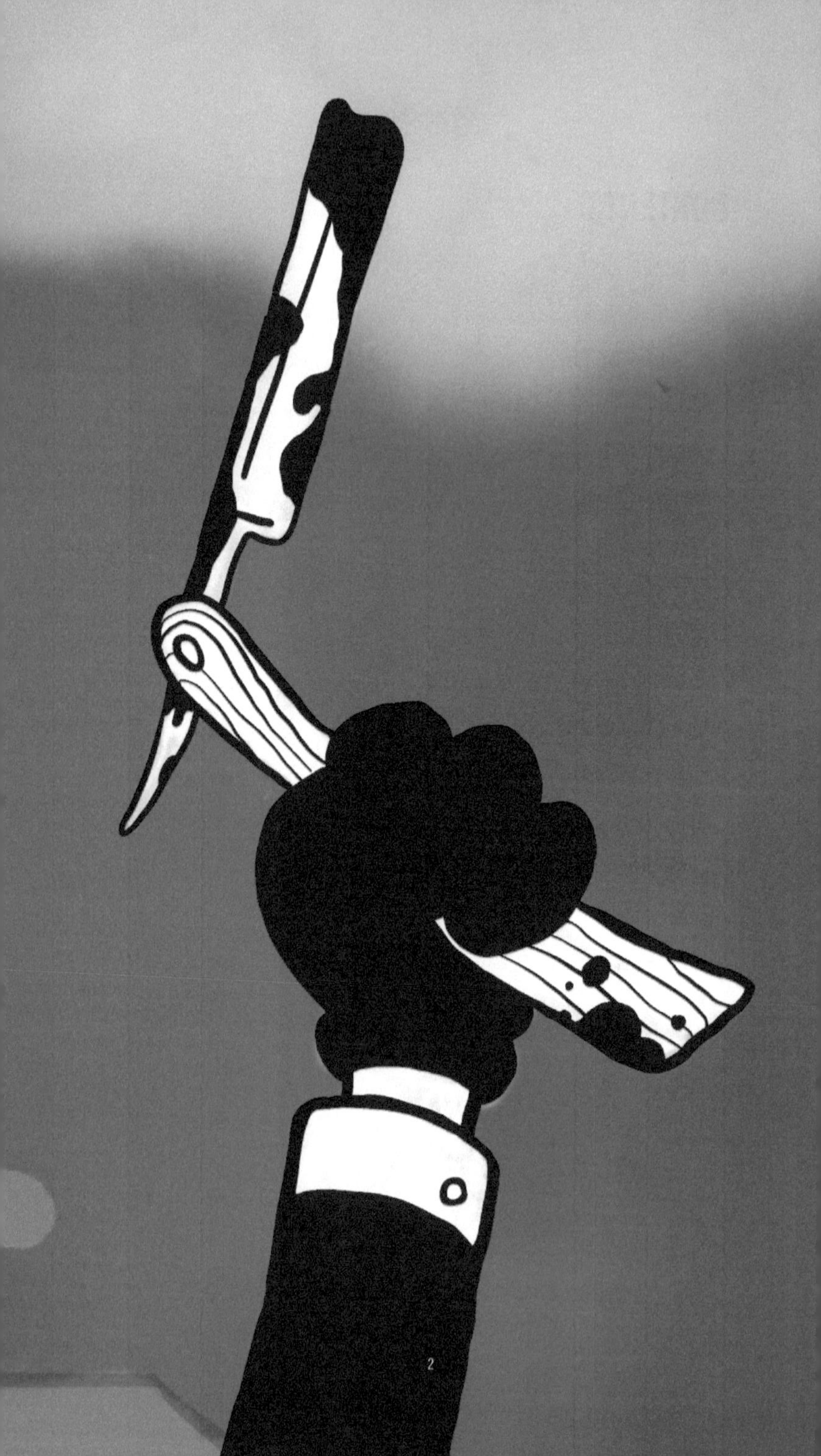

SICK
SICK
SICK

SICK SICK SICK

Achieving perfections
impostering arrogant waves.
Relieving infections
instinctively passing away.
Leaving in pieces
like parasites pounding their prey.
Believing this species
surrendered to simulate.

Lay down keep your eyes closed
and you'll be alright.
Guilty conscience consumes
all the daylight.
Maybe all your good deeds
will make the sun rise.
Maybe all your good deeds
will make the sun rise.

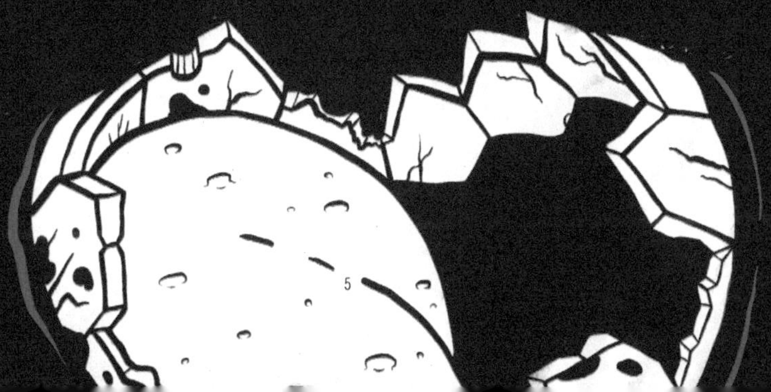

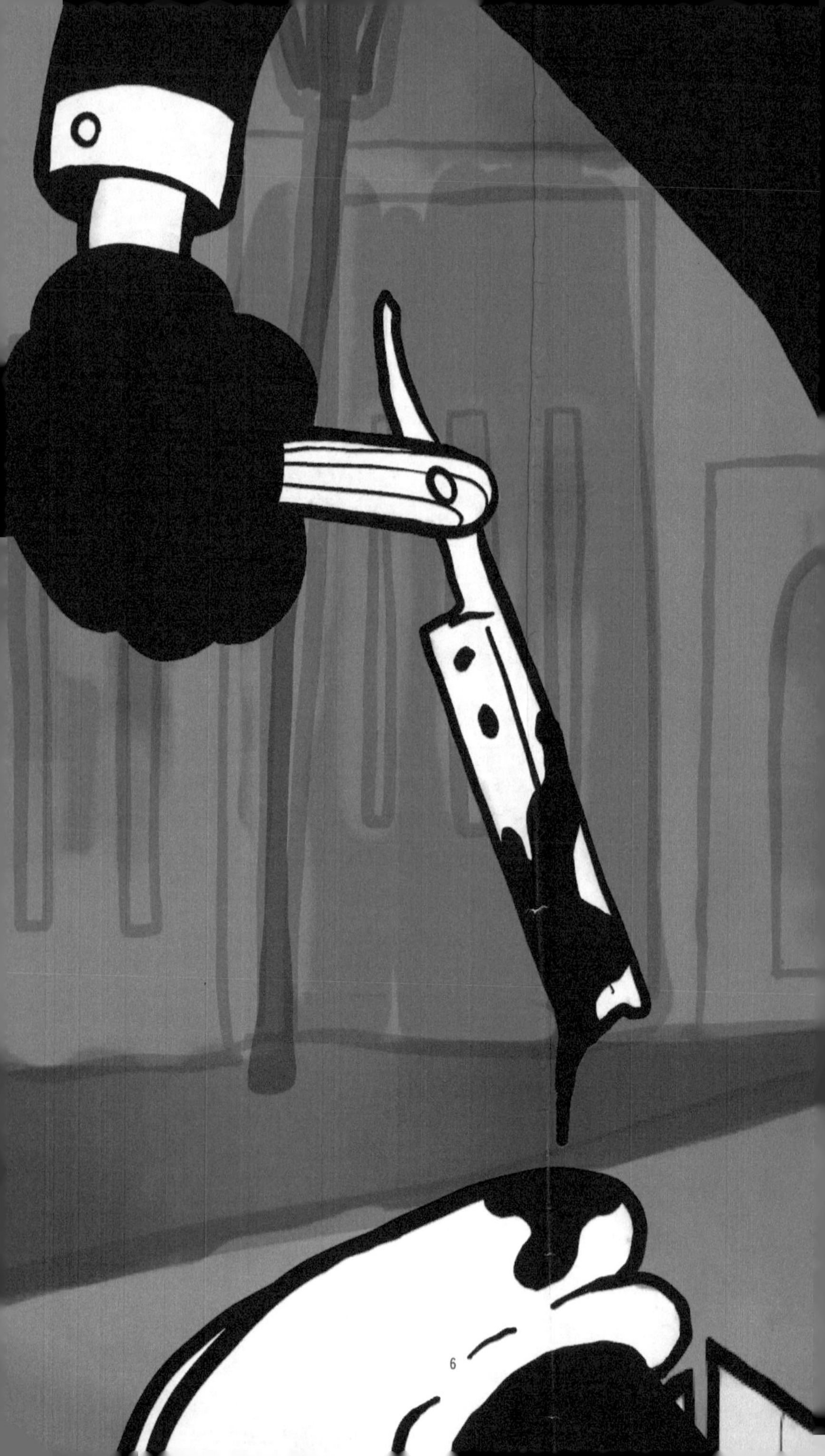

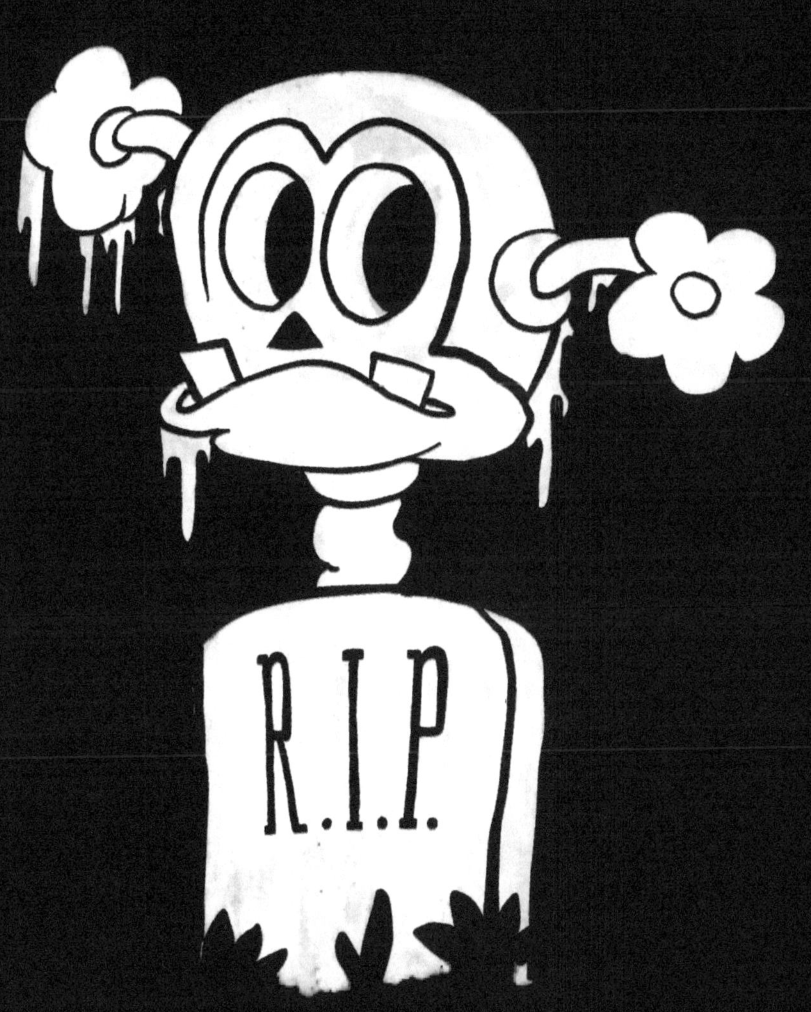
R.I.P.

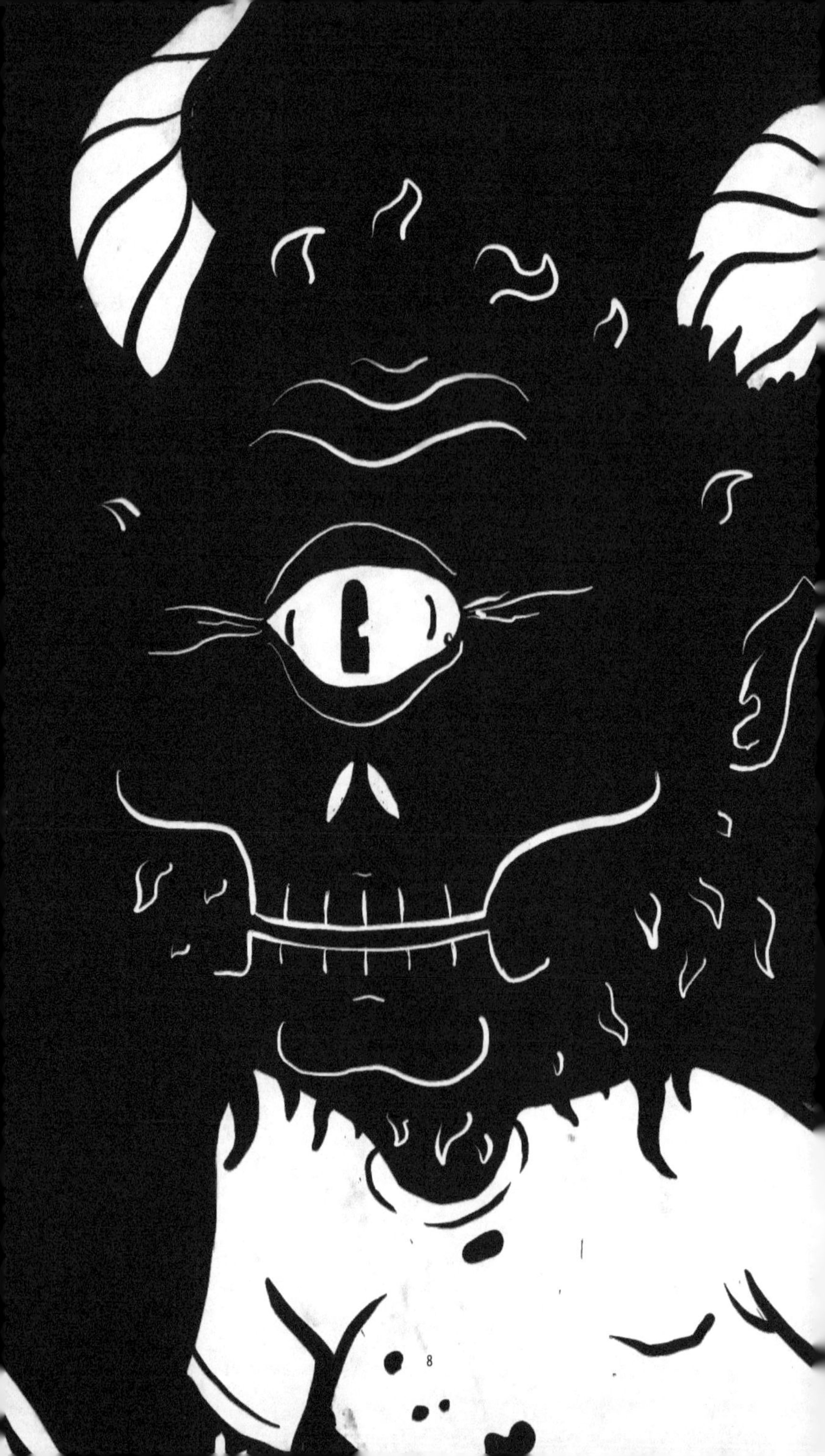

IT COMES IN THREE'S

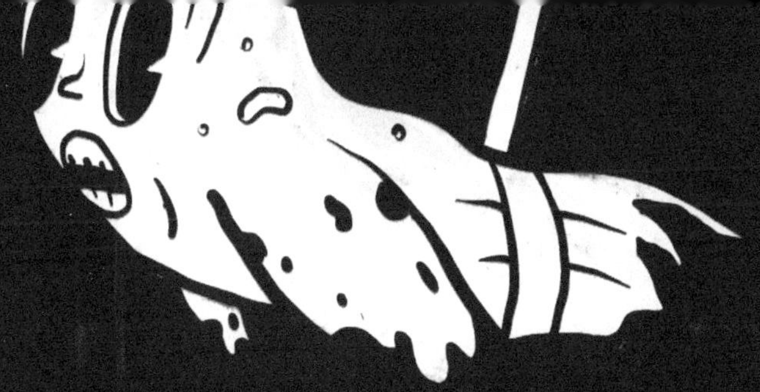

IT COMES IN THREE'S

Count the waves,
as they push right through.
And feel the sounds,
as they light the room.
And it comes in three's.

And your mouth stays dry,
'til you kiss the moon.
And you drink the life,
that the gods consume.
And it comes in three's

Slow breaths pull on time.
A second guess, the perfect line.
From below the stars are torn.
Sunlight cuts, the sky is born.

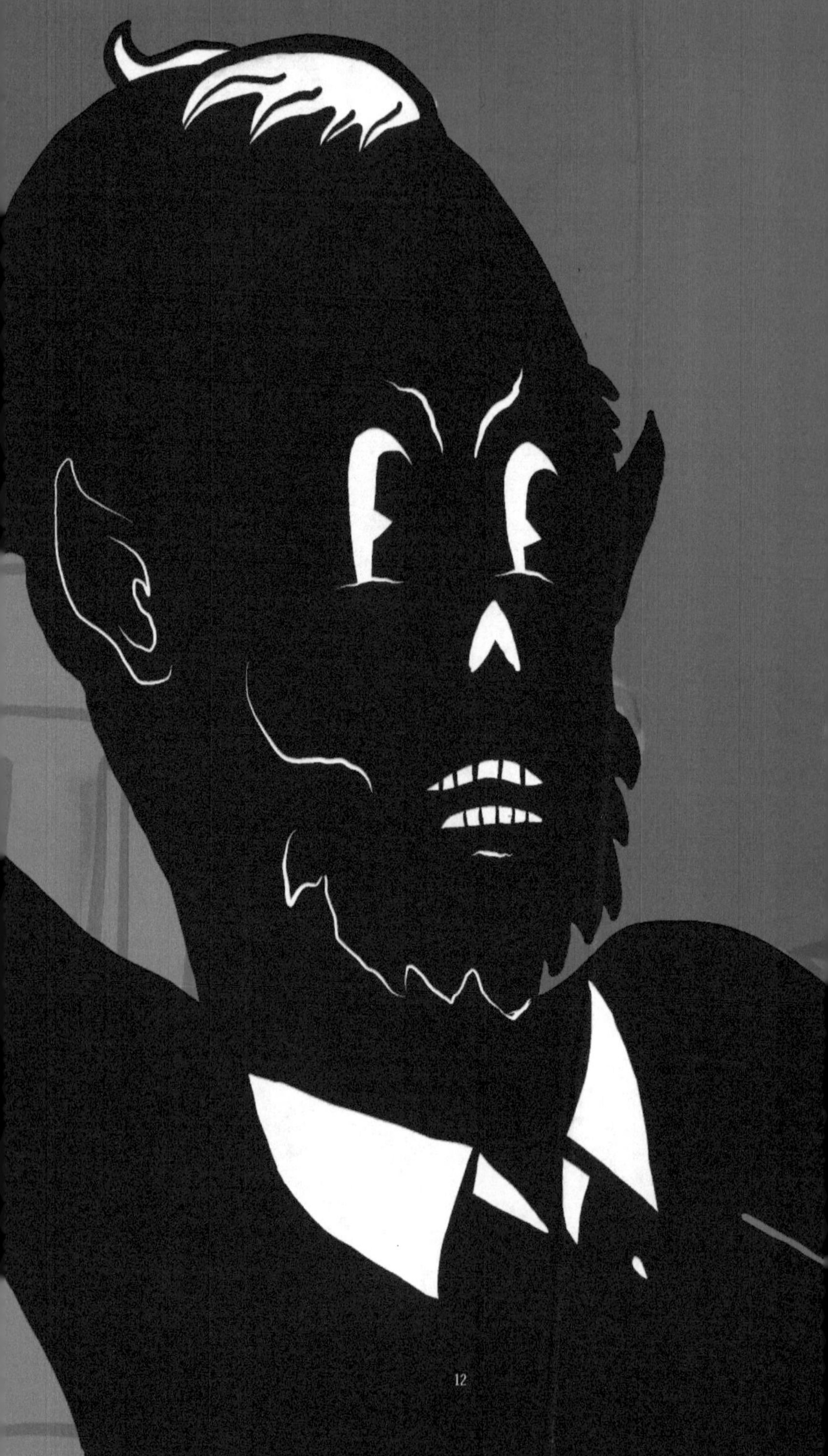

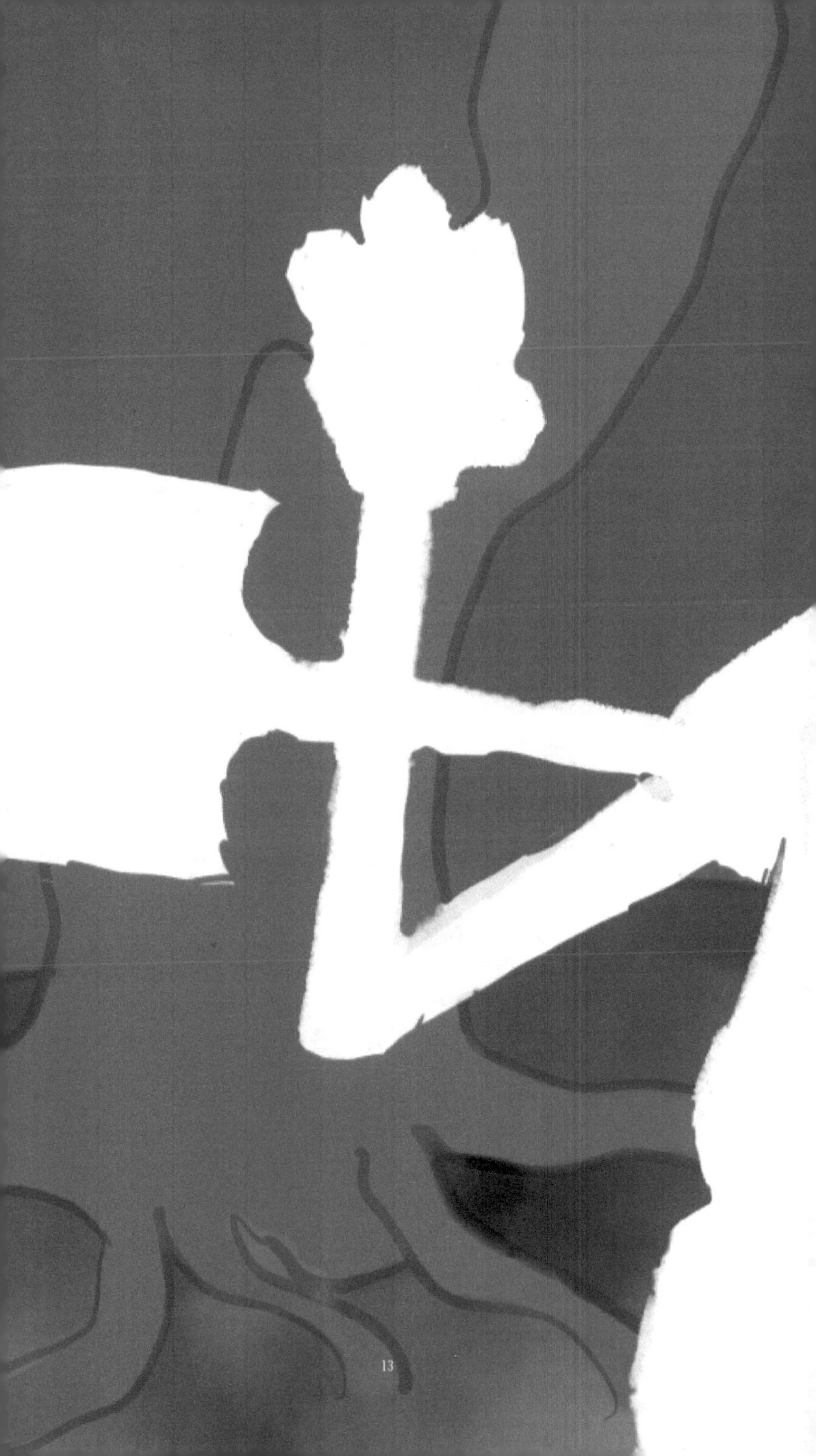

SILENT H

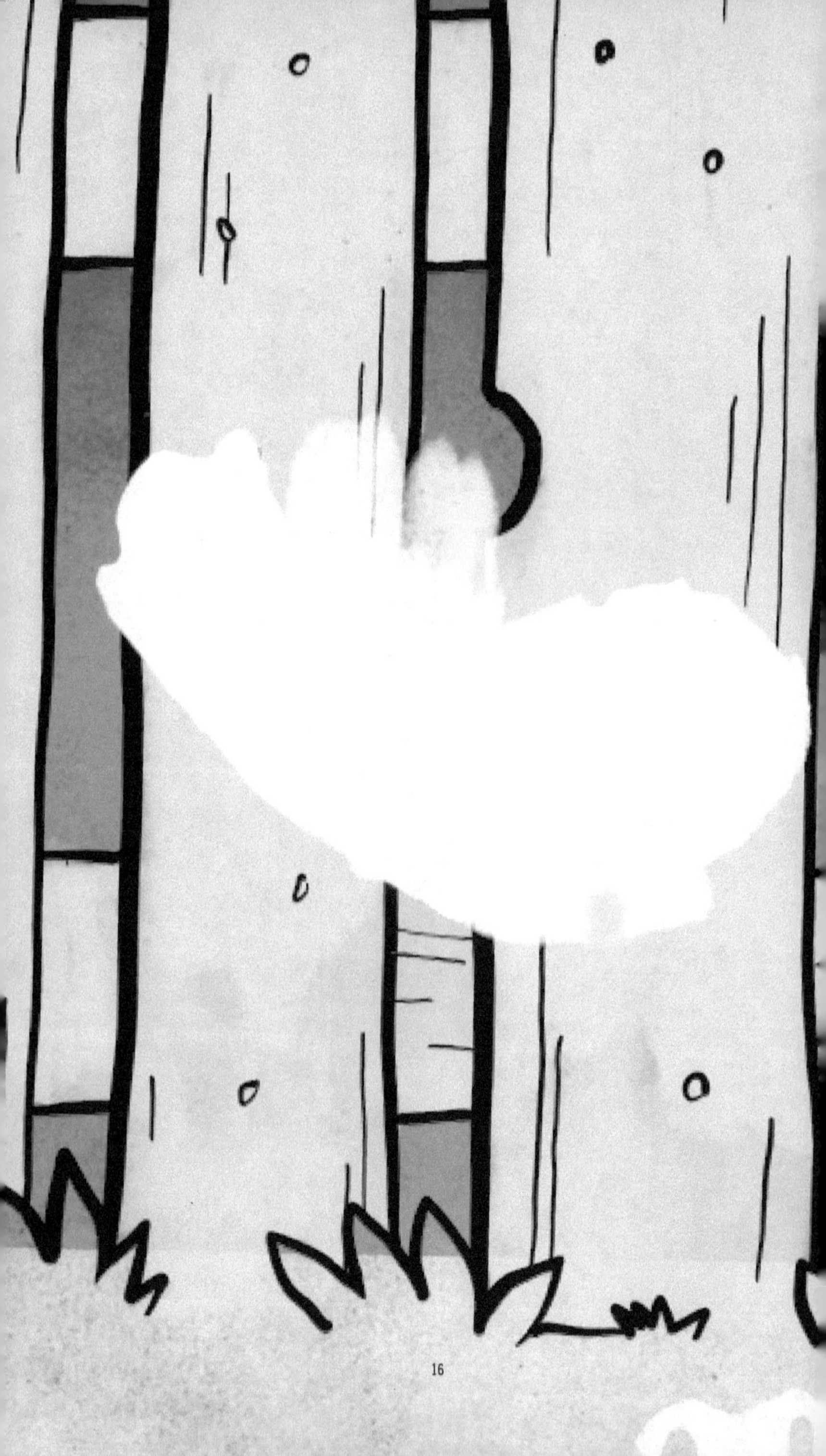

SILENT H

Climbed these walls
and never fell.
Except to lay beside me.
I believe, I believe, I believe
you're mine to keep.

Found the kills you left for me.
You chose to join the family.
I can see, I can see, I can see
you're mine to keep.

Twenty years a friend to me,
crush this world you're leaving.
I can see the sympathy
that I know youre giving me.
Lay your head down on the rug.
As the last breath leaves your lungs.
Friend to me, friend to me,
friend you're always.

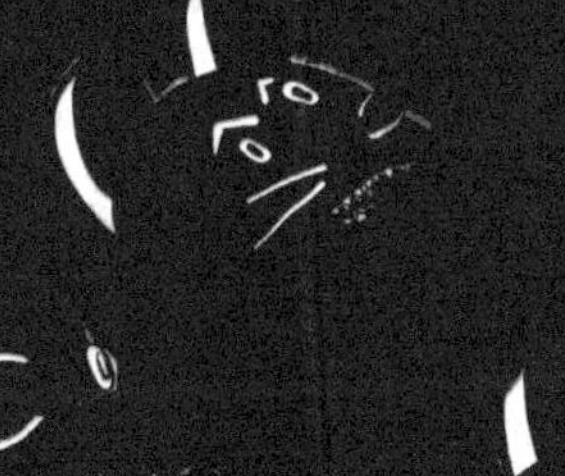

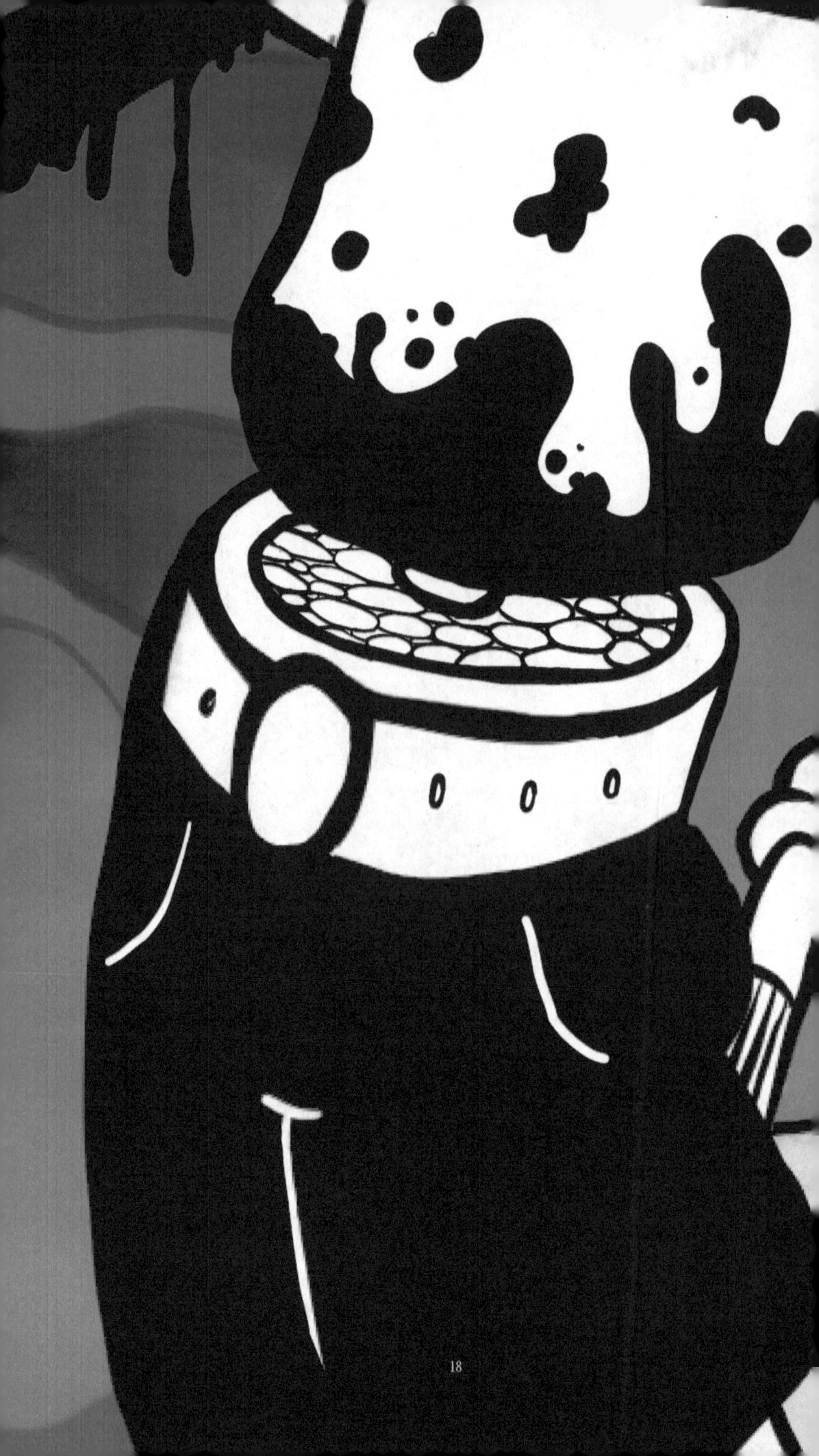

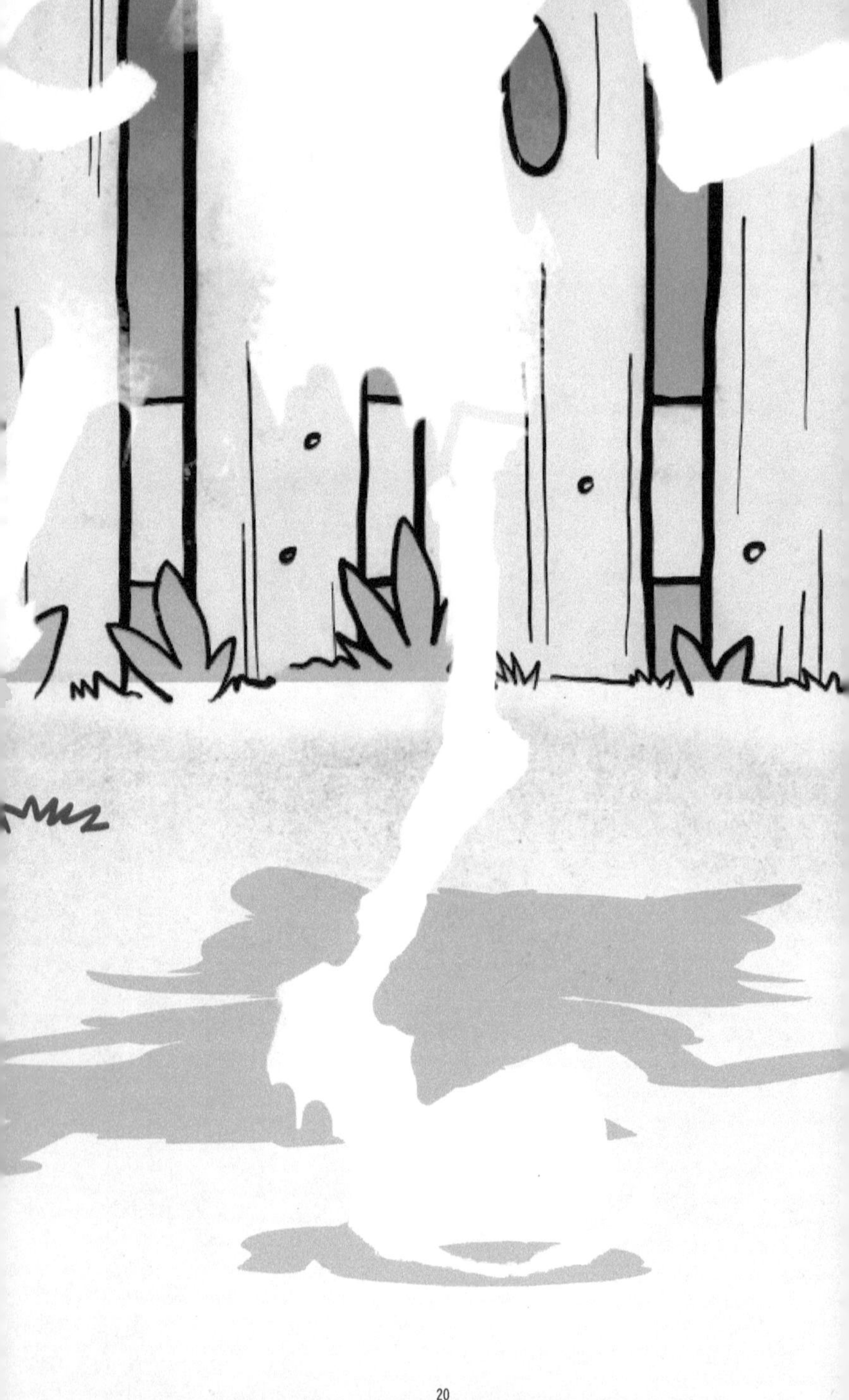

CHOKE ON IT

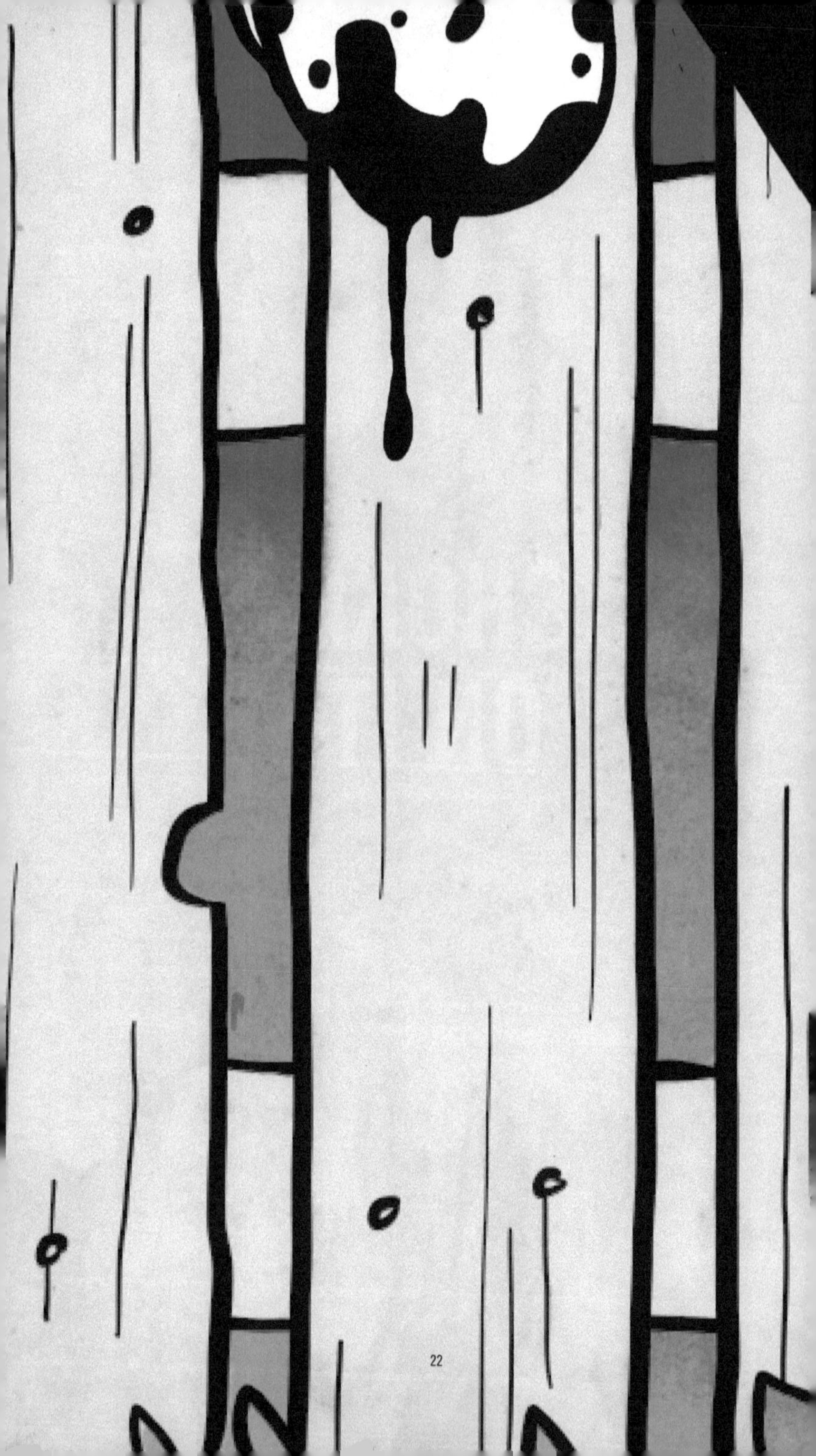

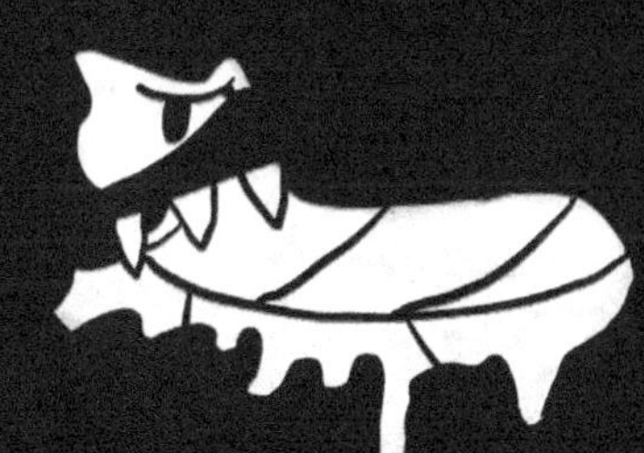

CHOKE ON IT

Been too long. Need to quit.
Hold it in. Choke on it
I know I hate myself.
Stop this circle.
Fighting these flaws is like
following fireflies.
Finding fatigue as they're
finally flying by.
Feeling fucked up
and I know it's fucked up
but I just repeat it.
Hold my breath, maybe it stops churning.
Hold my world, maybe it stops turning.
Hold my tongue, making my way down.
Hold my hand, maybe I'll wait it out.
Choke on it.

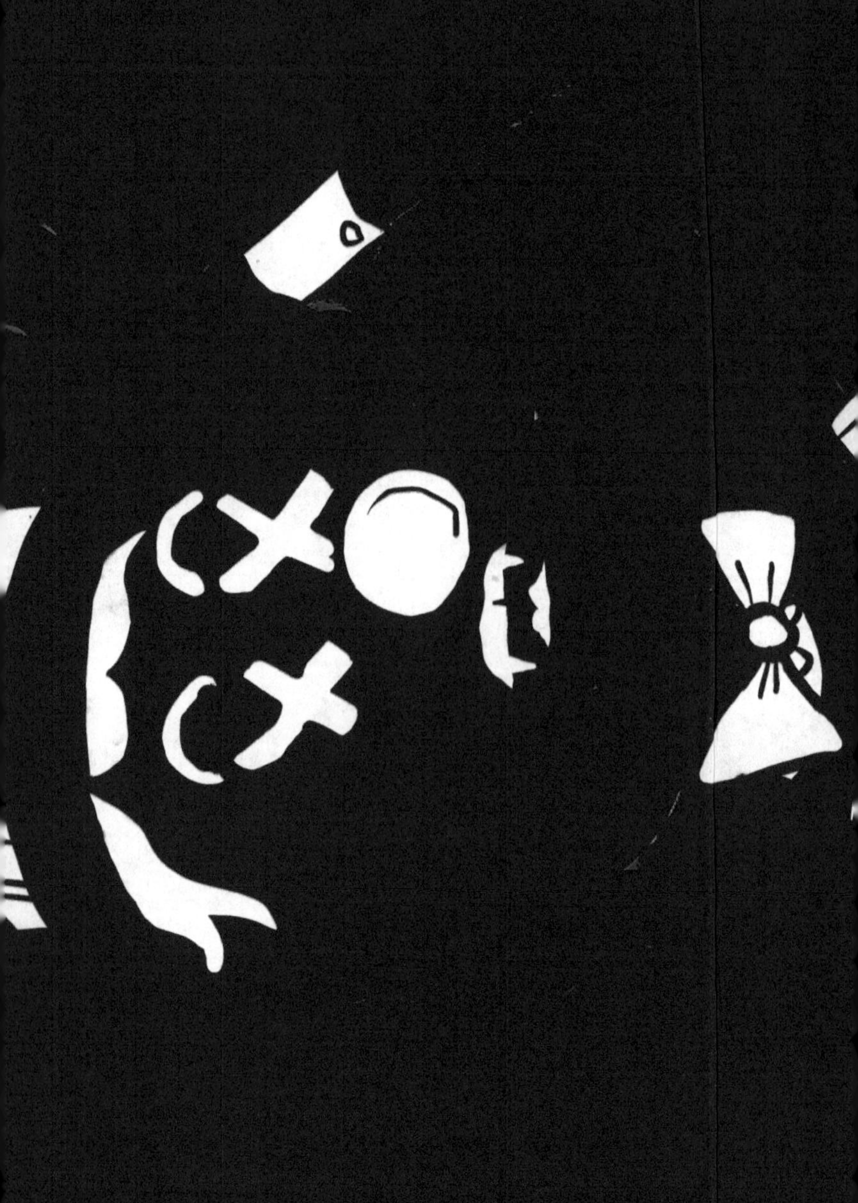

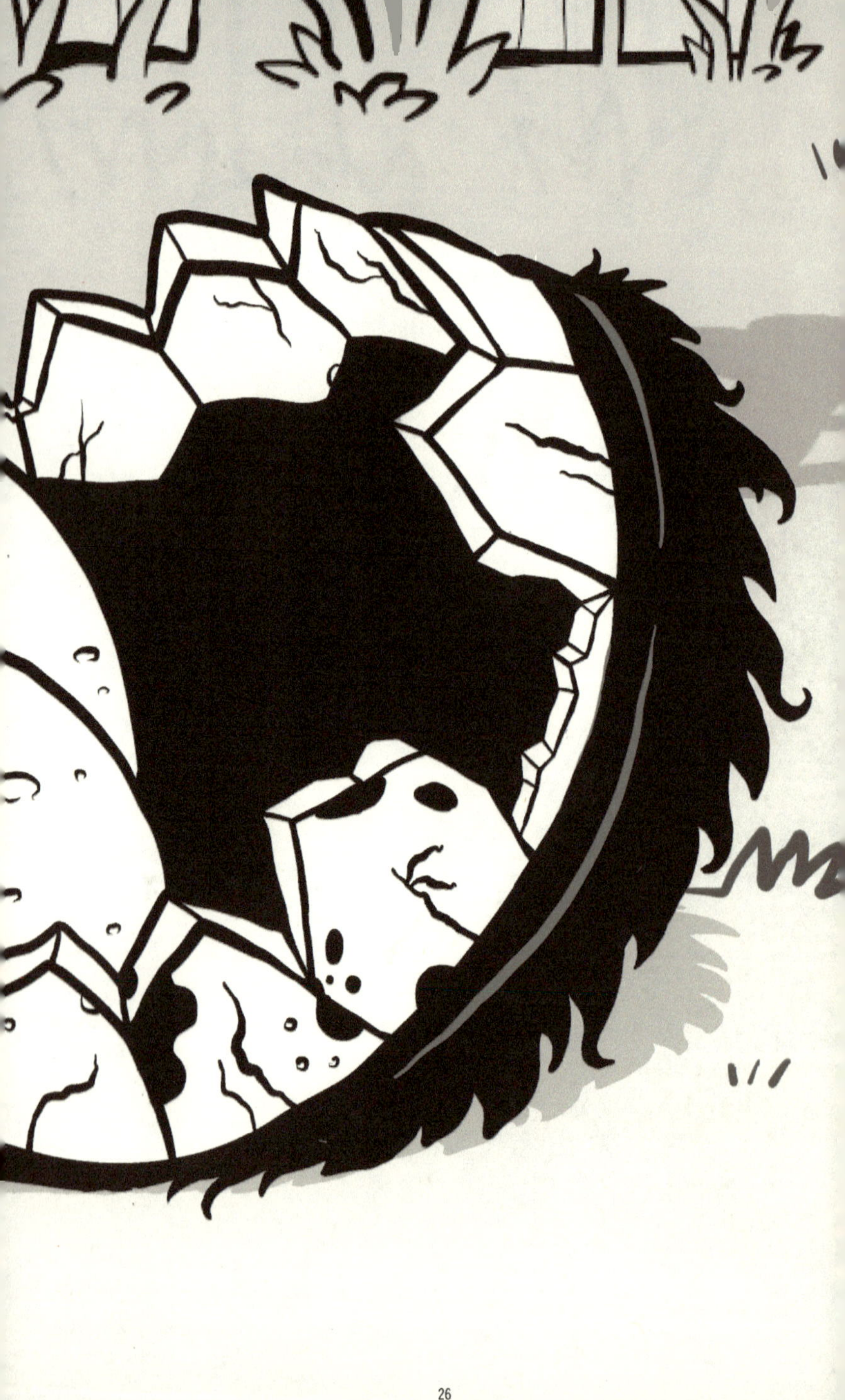

RESIDUAL MADNESS

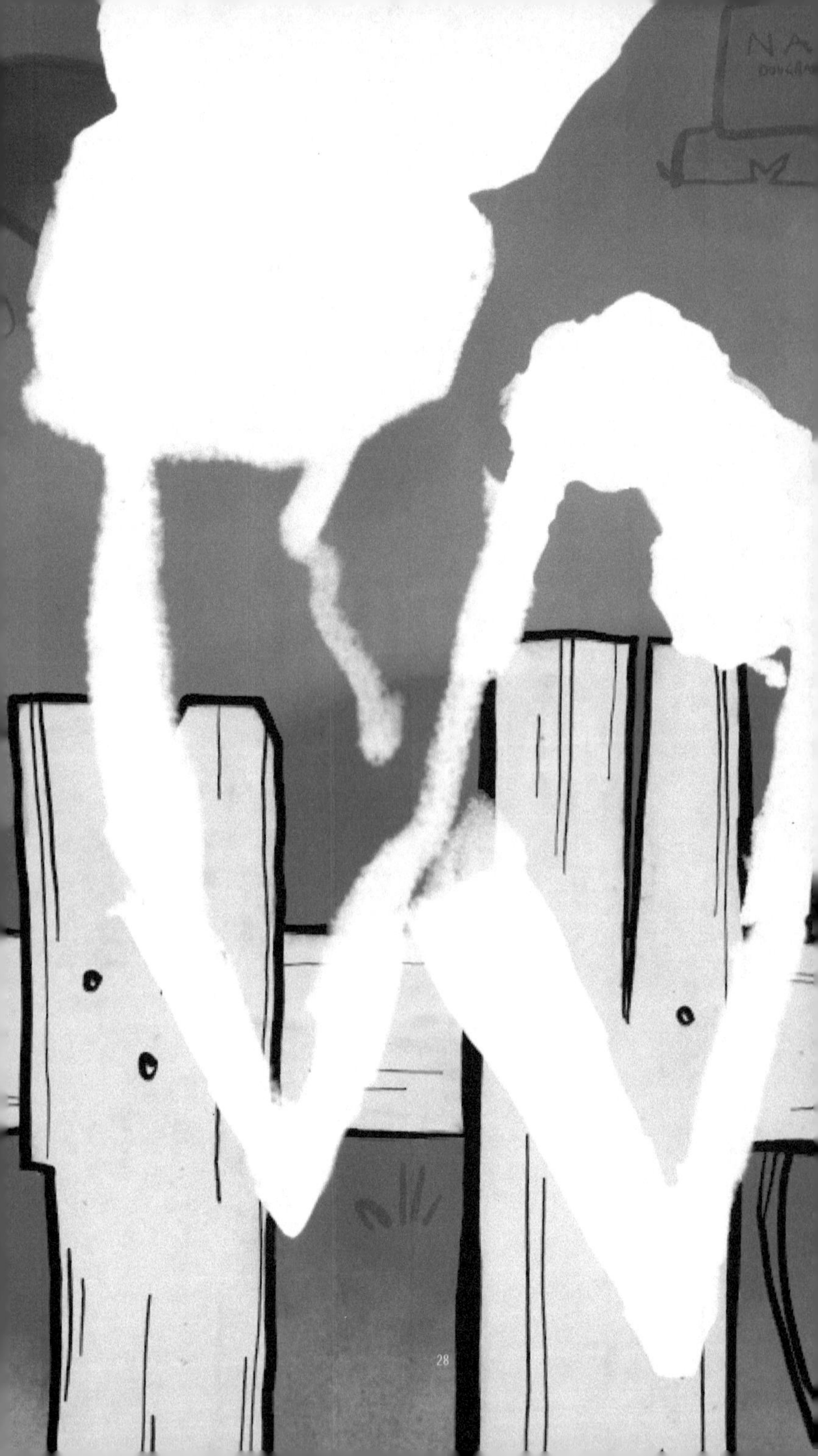

RESIDUAL MADNESS

Put that finger
on the trigger.
This cannot be real.
Stuck in this space
as I start to erase
and I'll never know
how to feel.

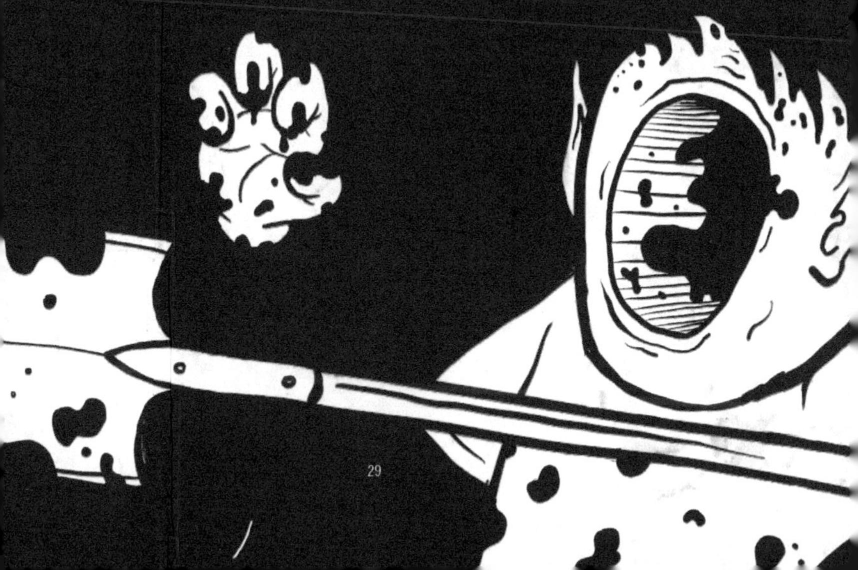

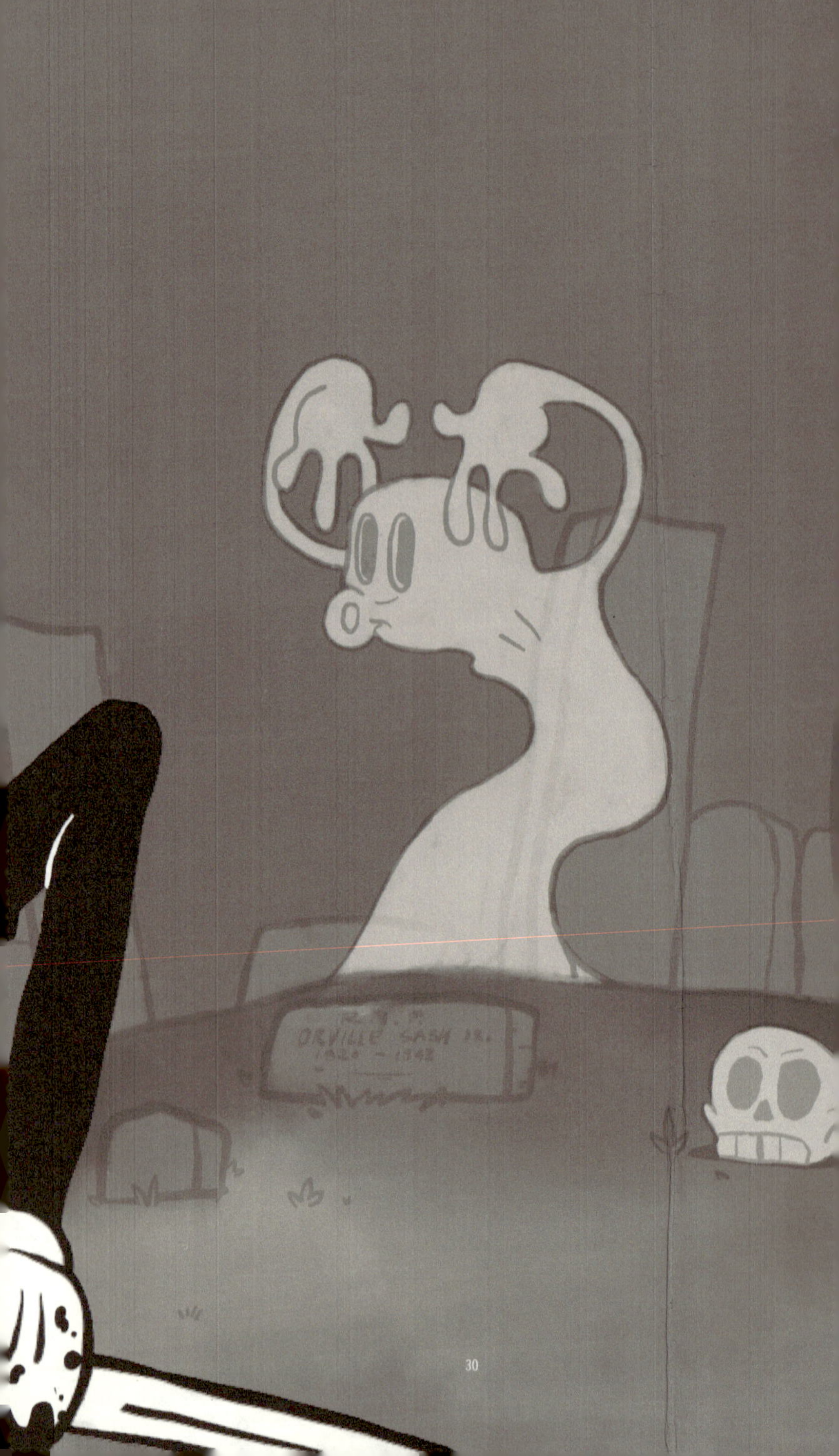
ORVILLE SASH JR.

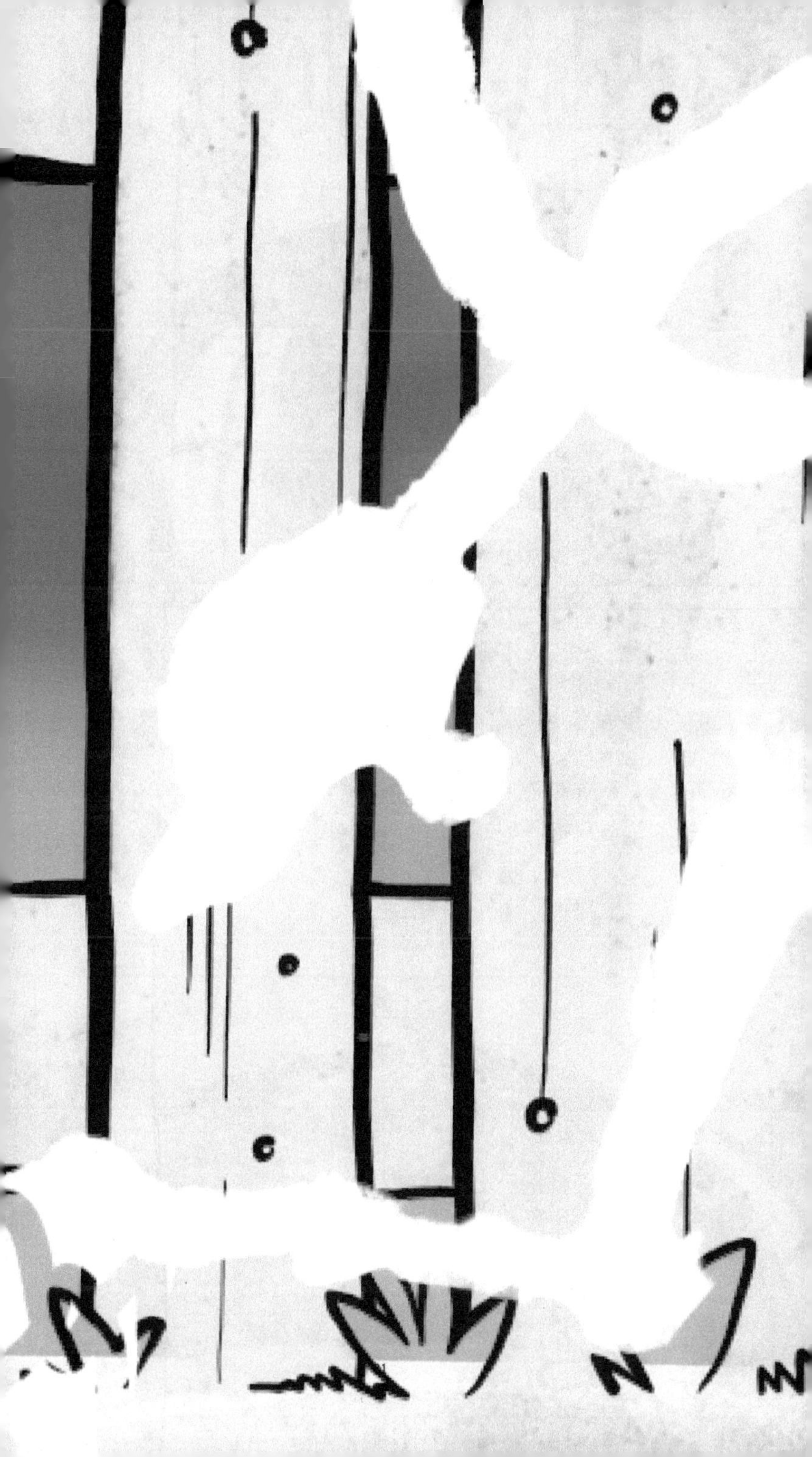

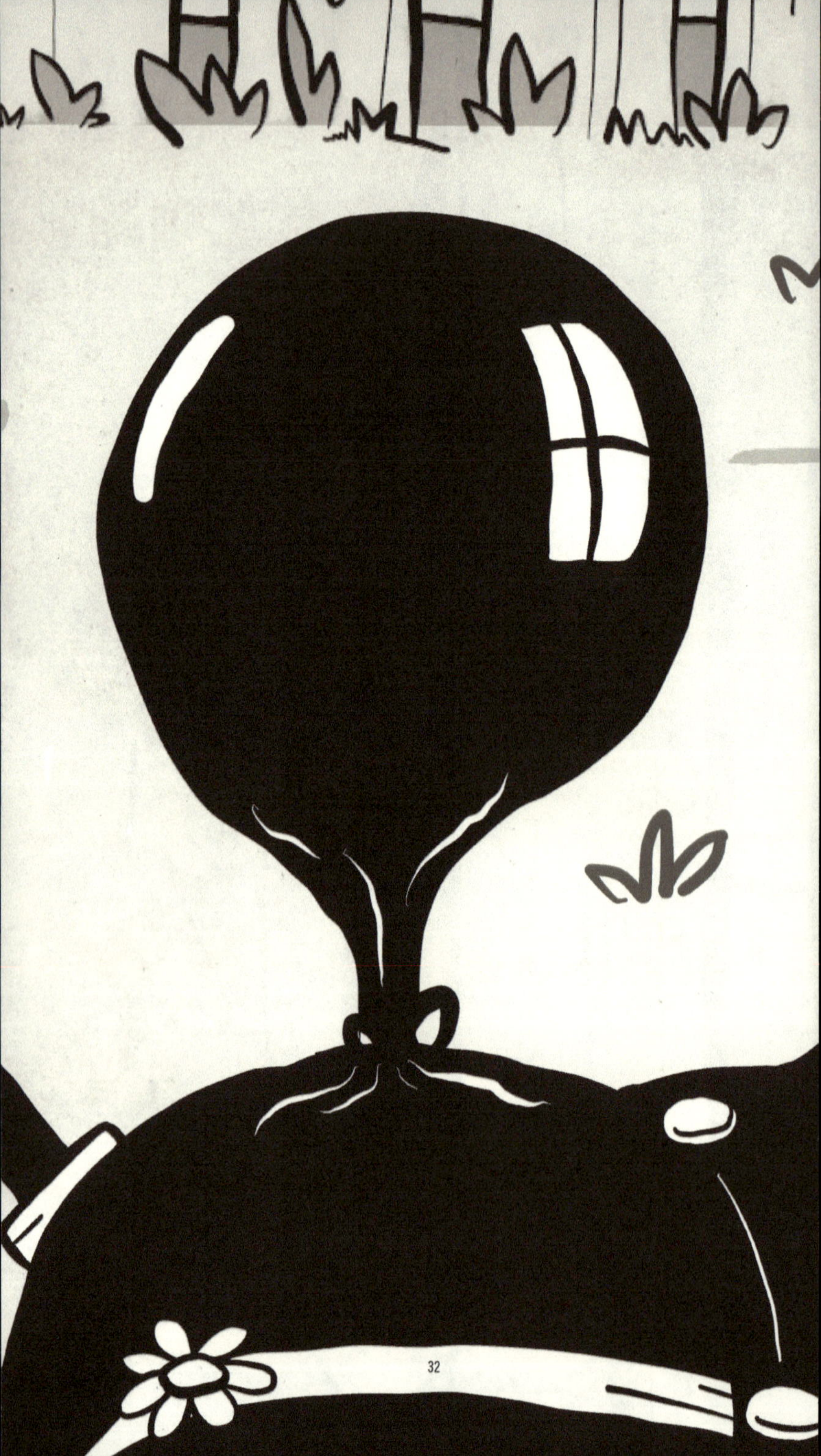

DROWN

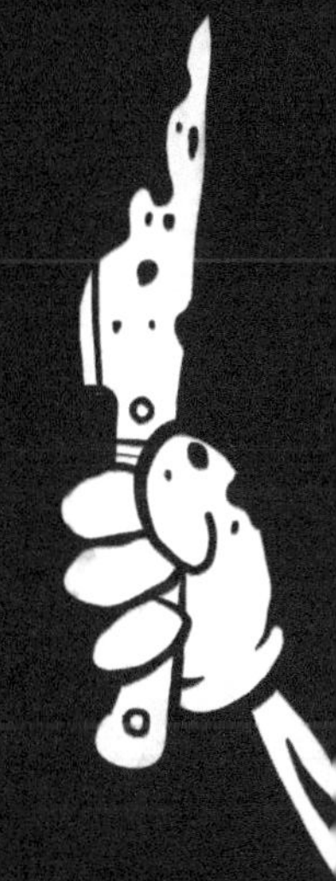

DROWN

Drown
It's alright,
It's over,
You can't fight back
Drown

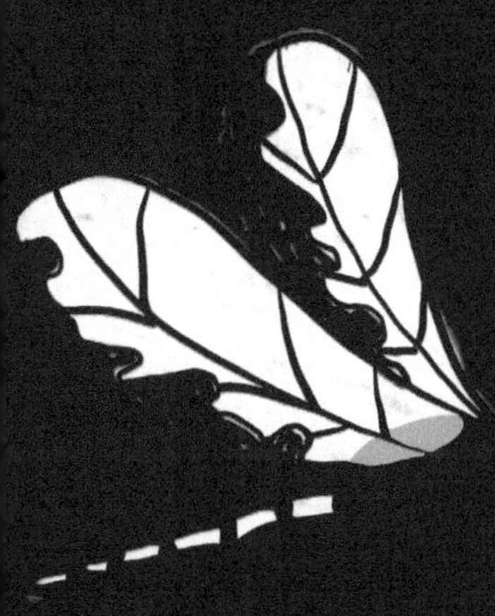

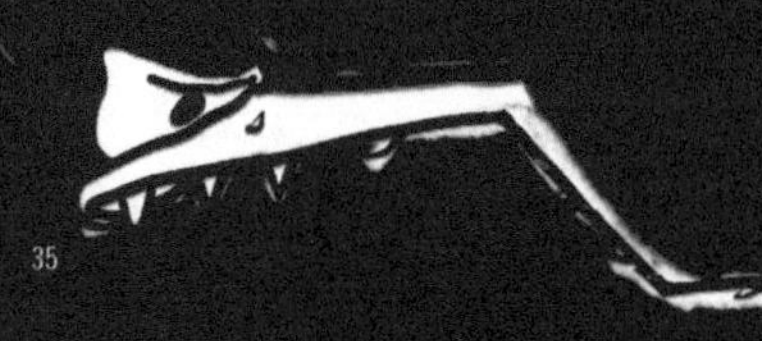

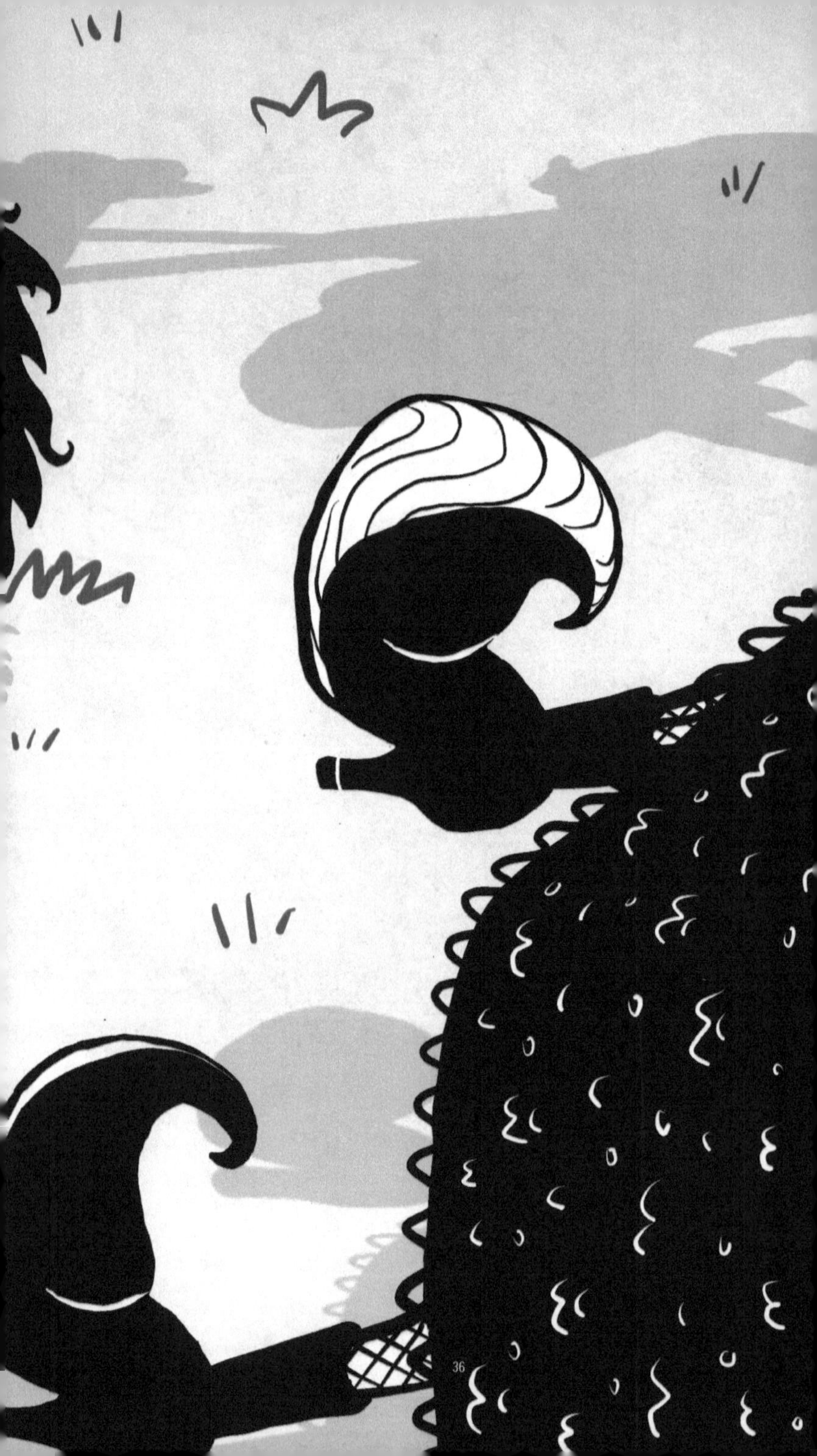

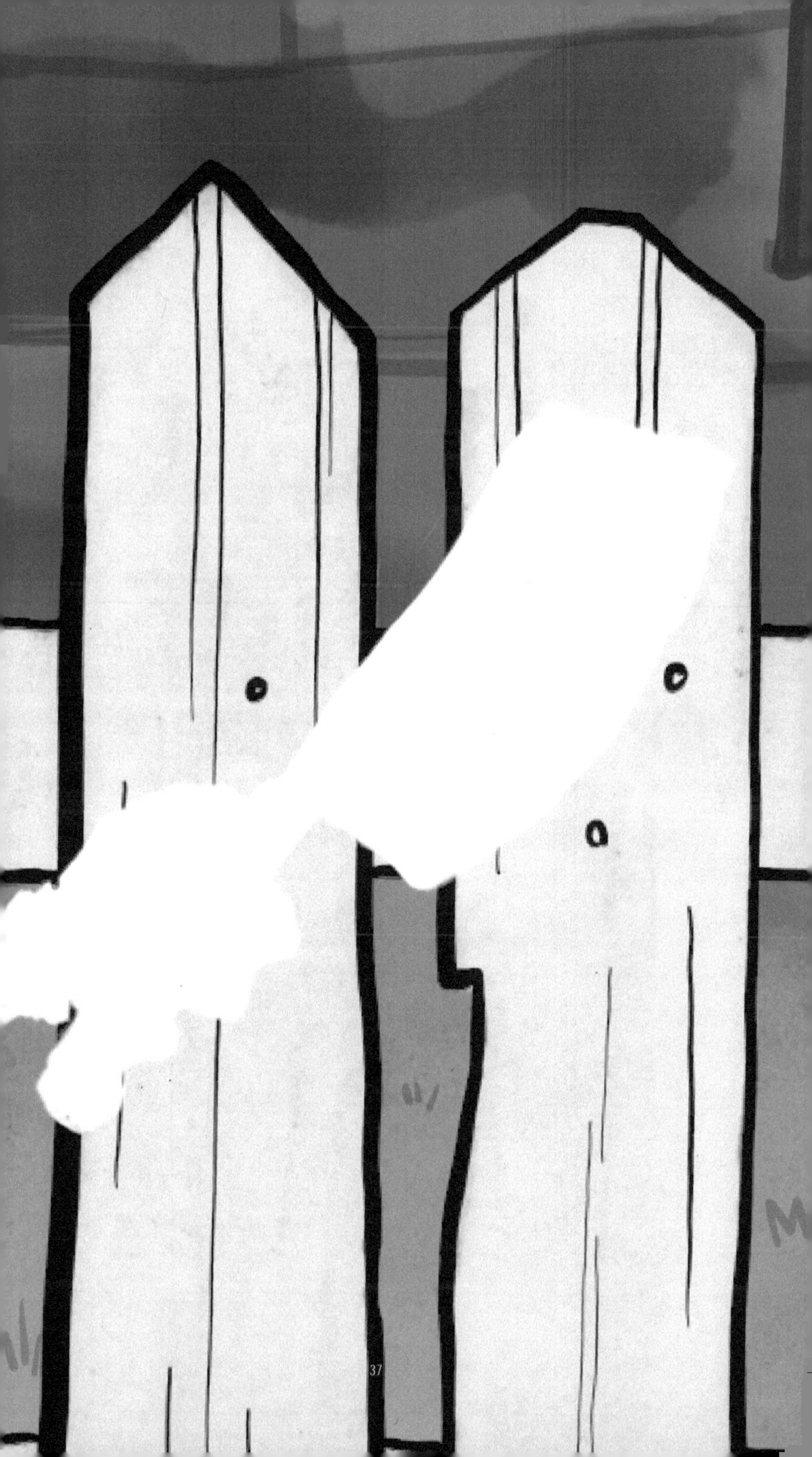

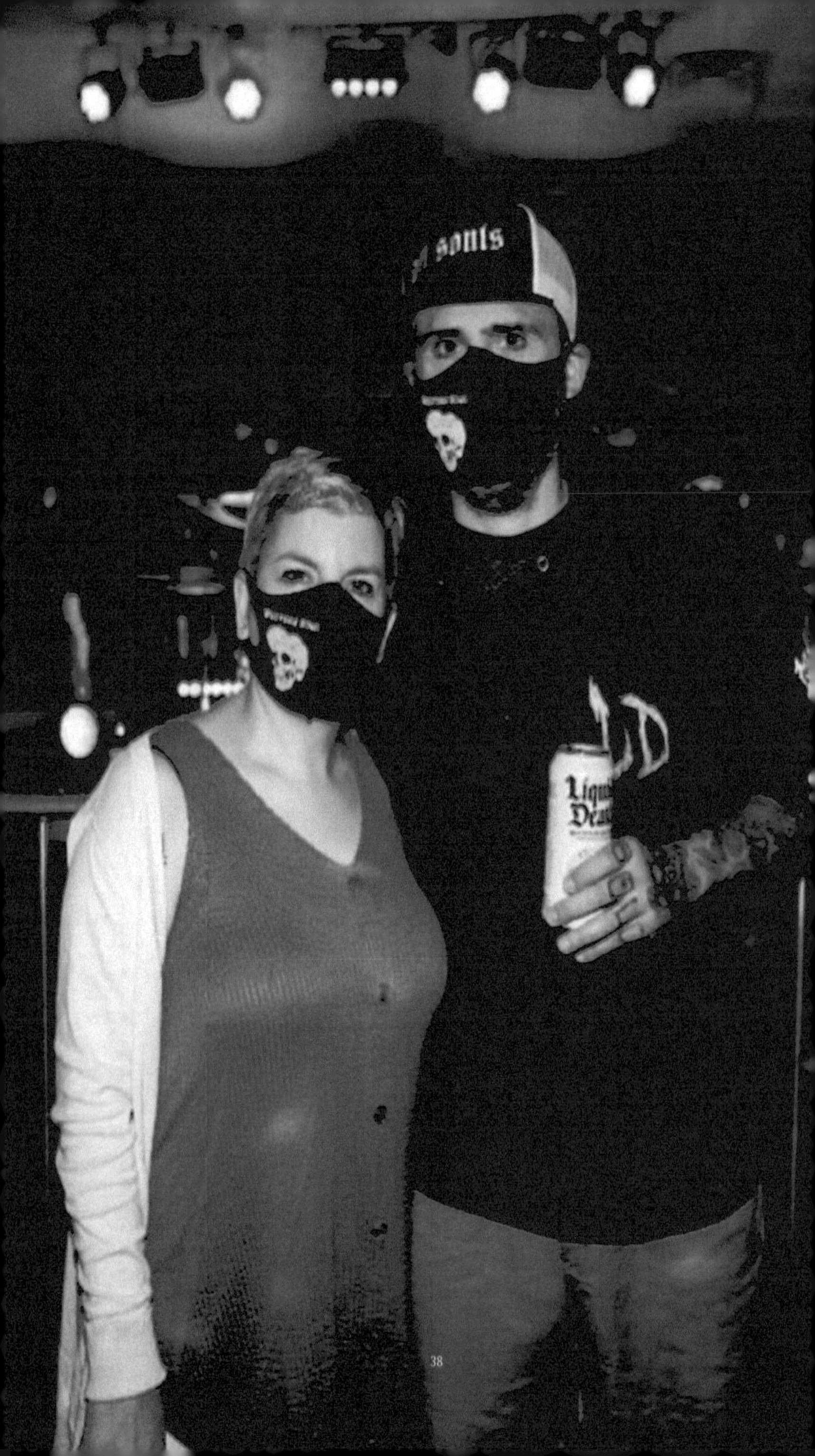
Sons

WESTSIDE BOWL

Our home base, our second home, and our family. The Offerdahls and the entire staff at the WSB are a huge part of our lives. It's where we filmed our videos for Starved and Choke On It.

Endless thanks to everyone involved, and to all that support this amazing venue in our hometown. None of this would be possible without you.

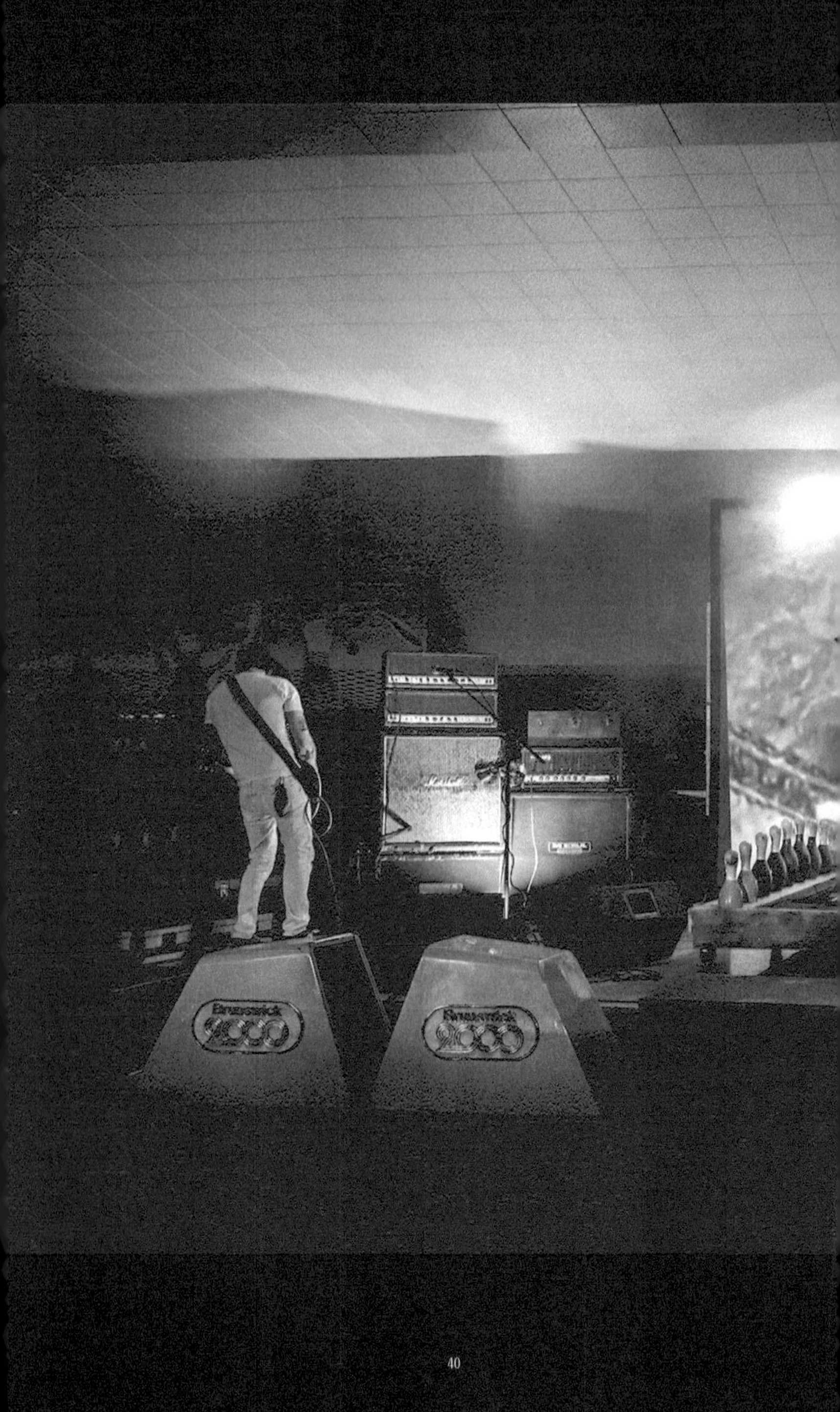
Brunswick
Brunswick

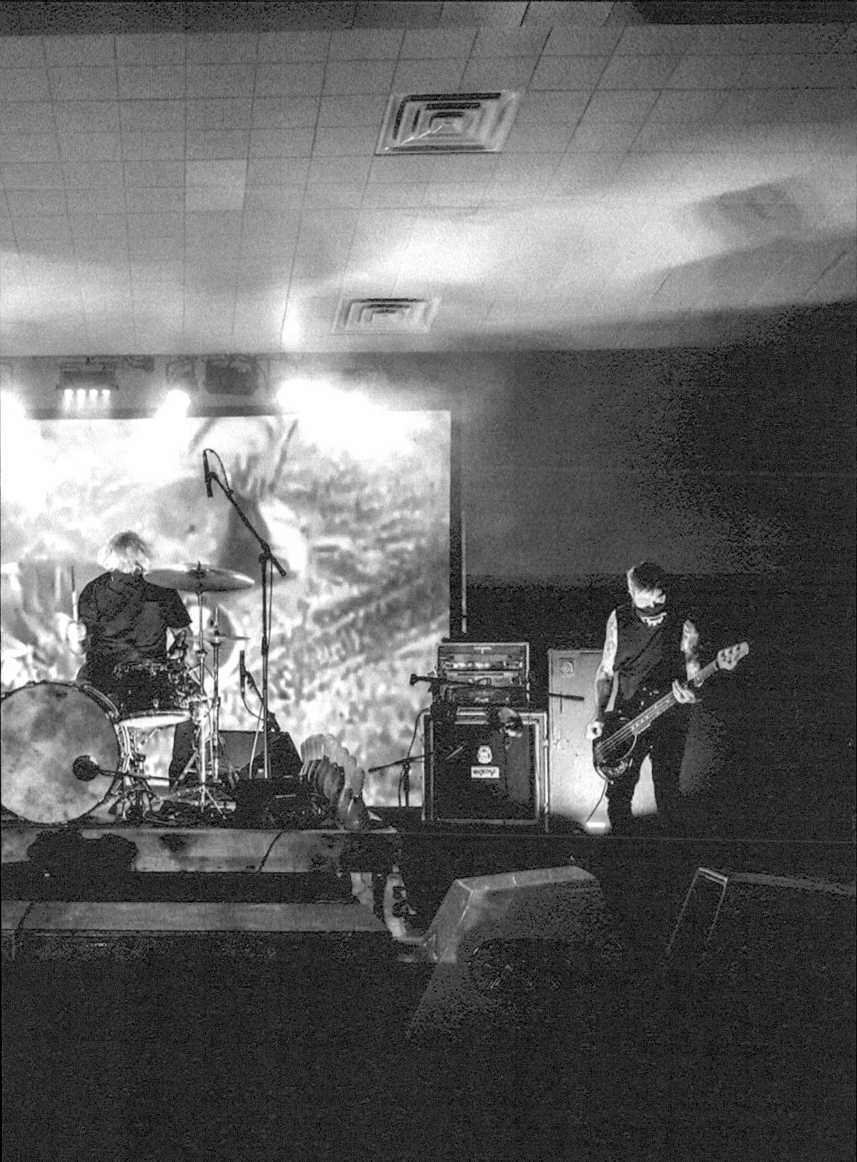

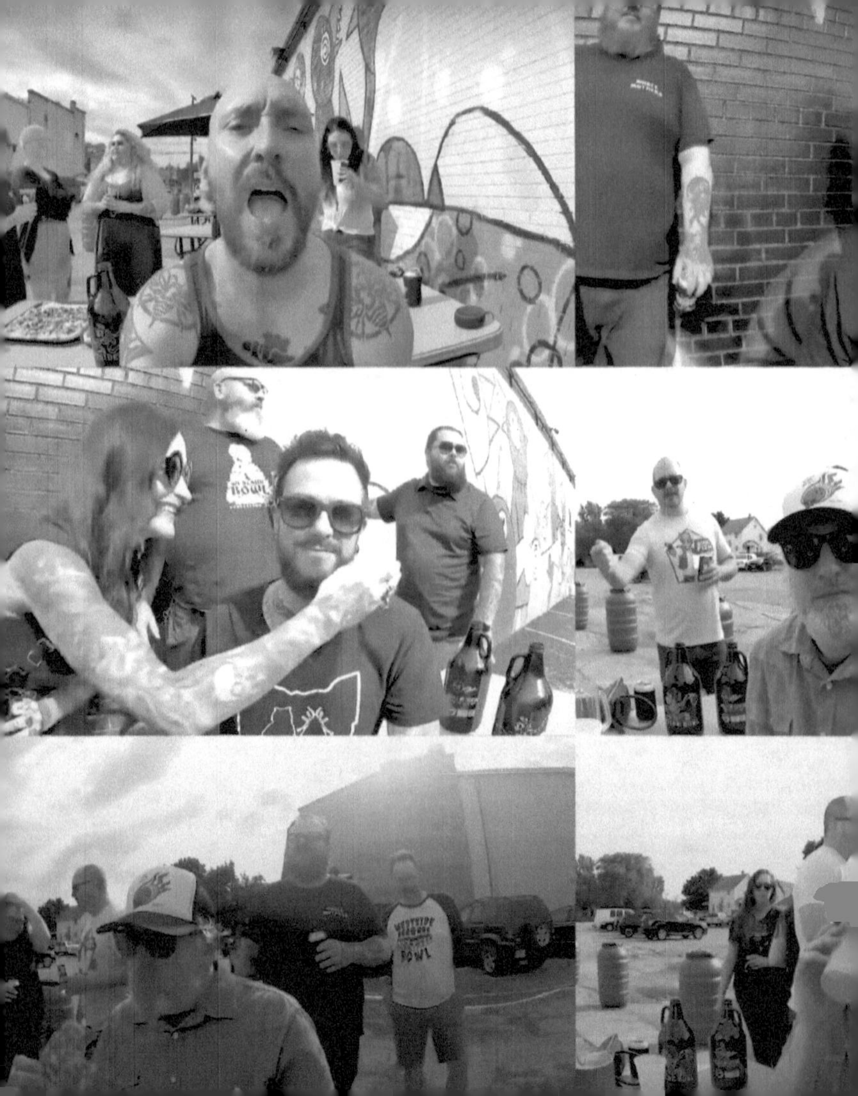
BOWL
BOWL

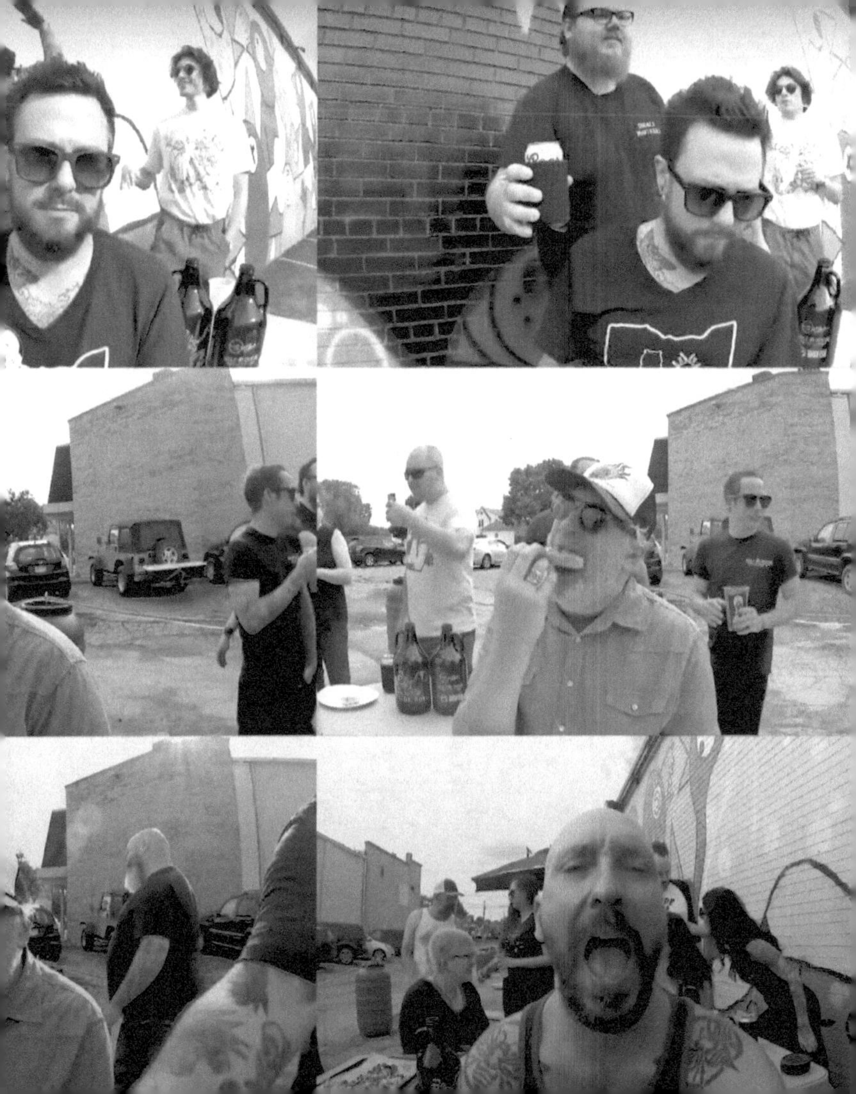

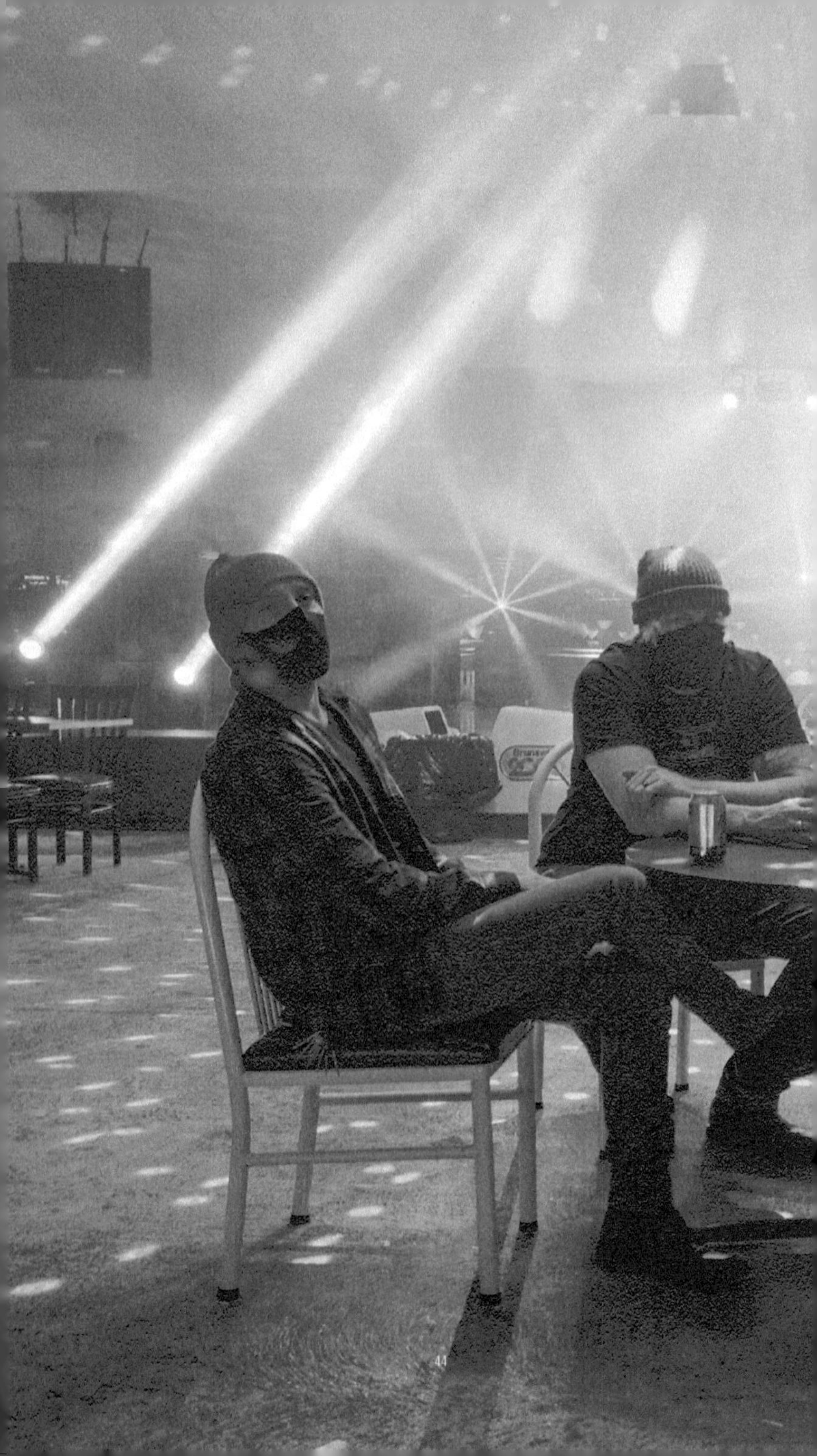

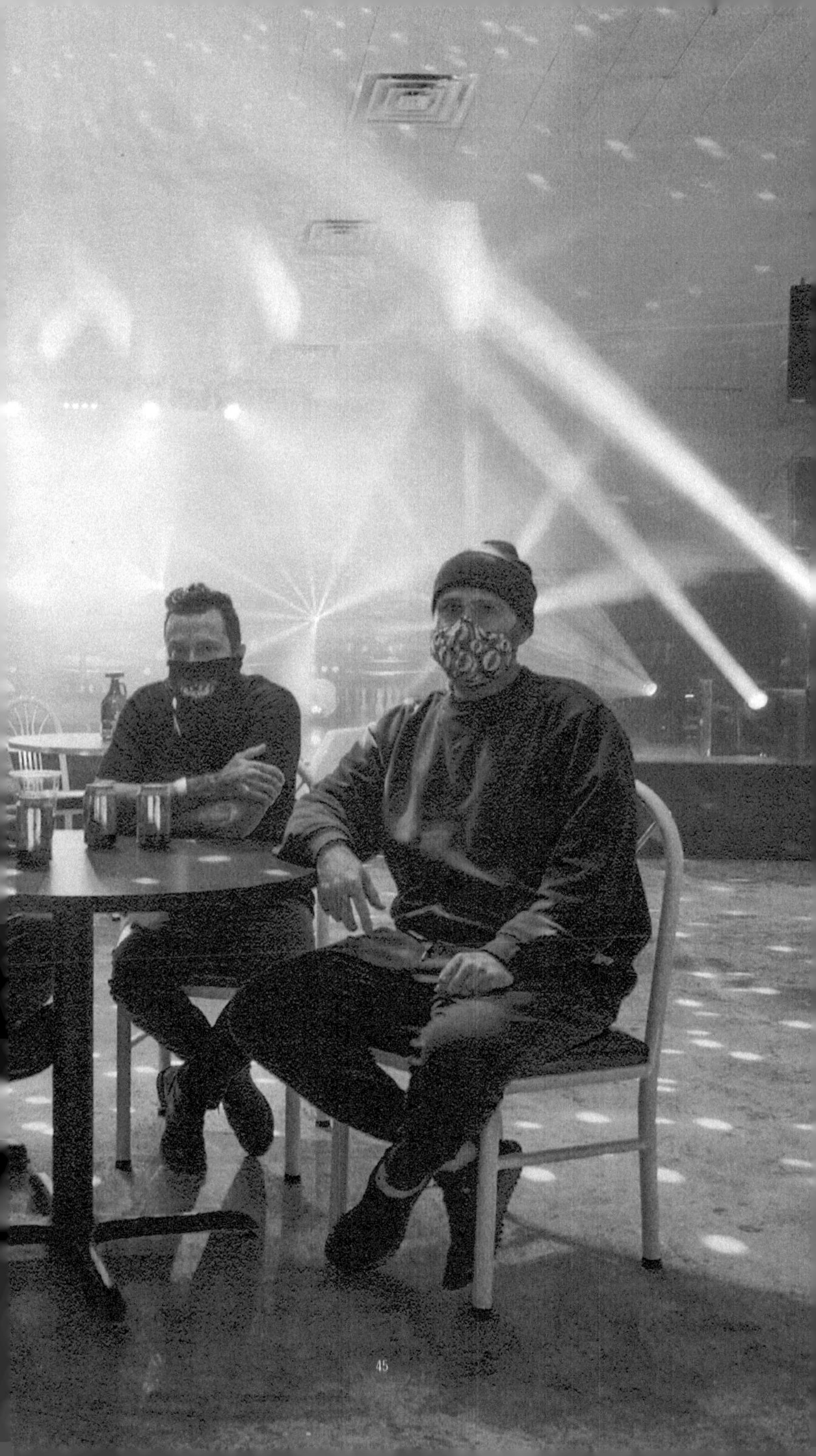

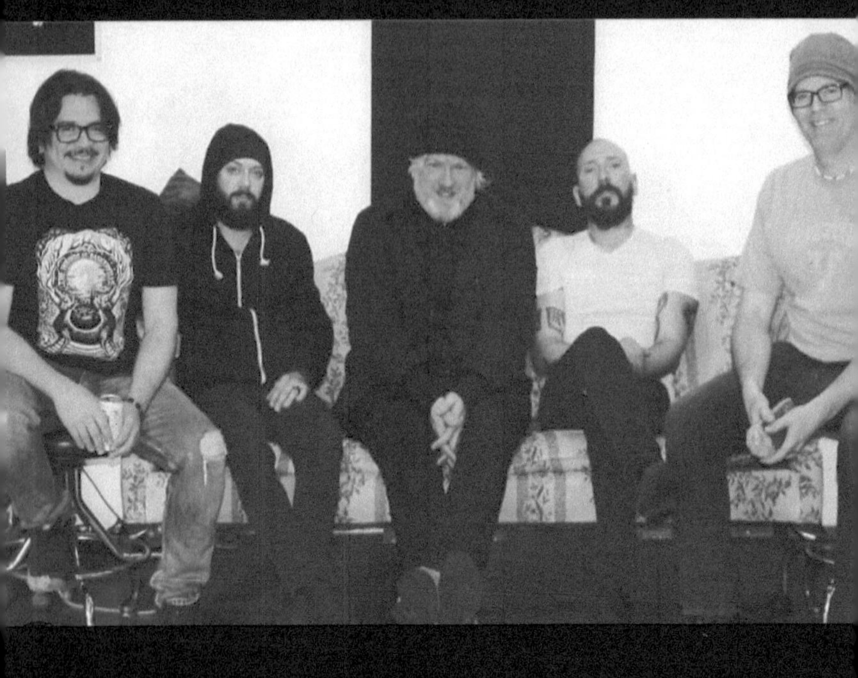

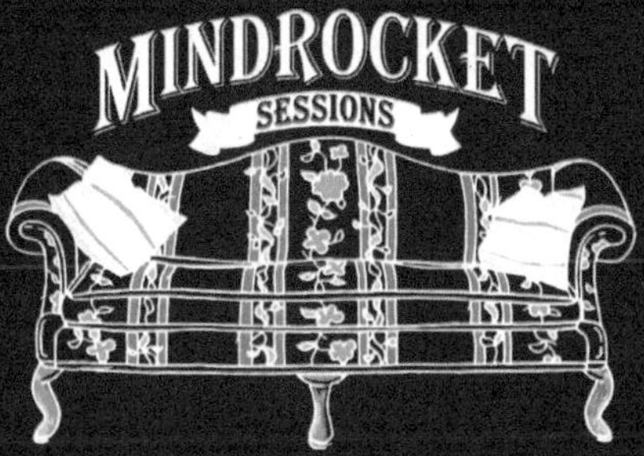

MIND ROCKET
RECORDING STUDIO

Working with Josh Roman and Mindrocket Recording studio has always been a pleasure for us. Josh goes way back with Rebreather and knows our sound better than anyone. His decades of expertise shine through each and every time we work together.

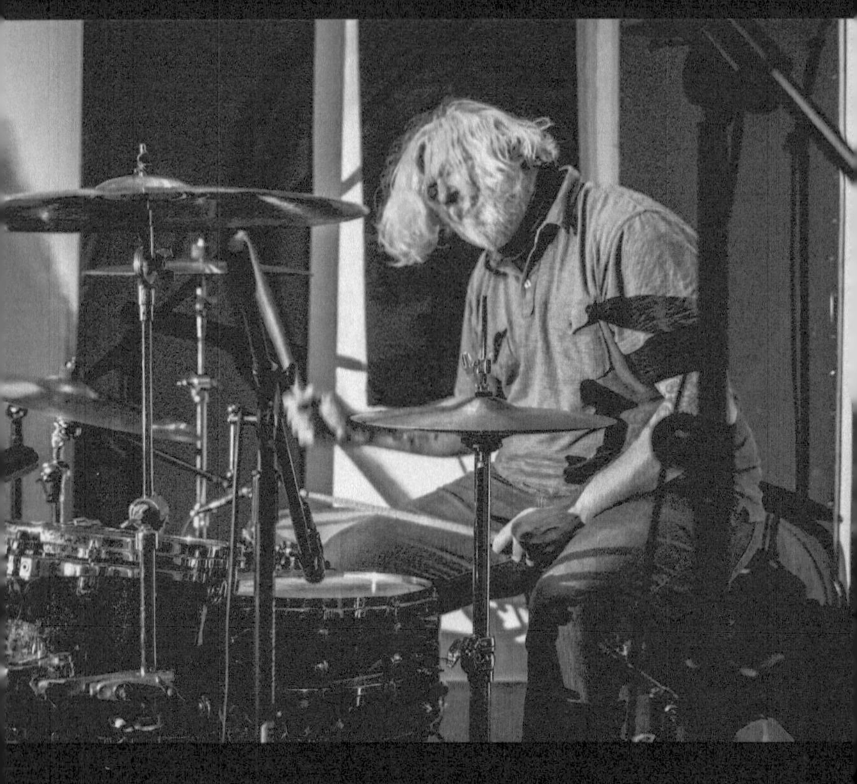

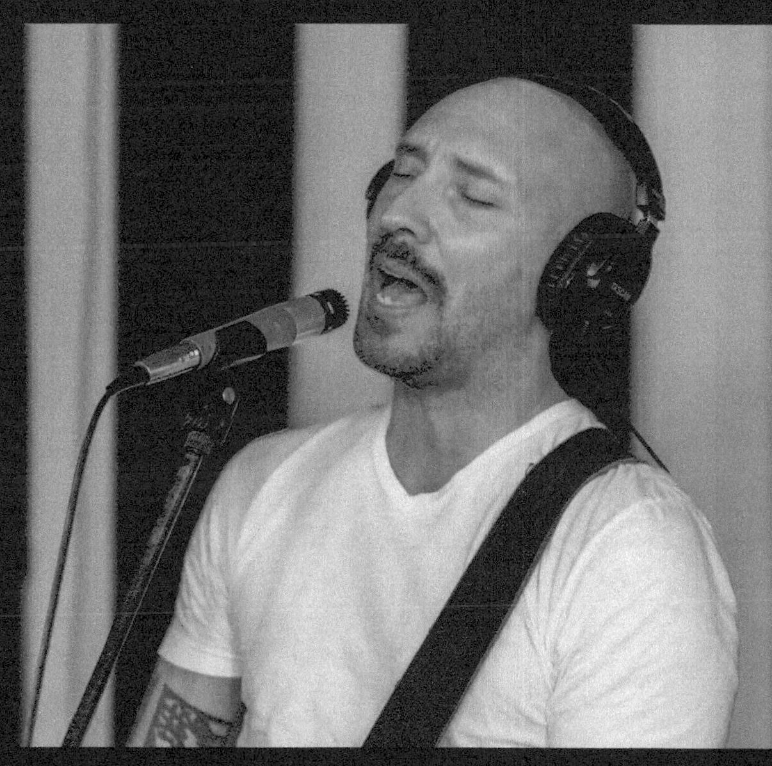

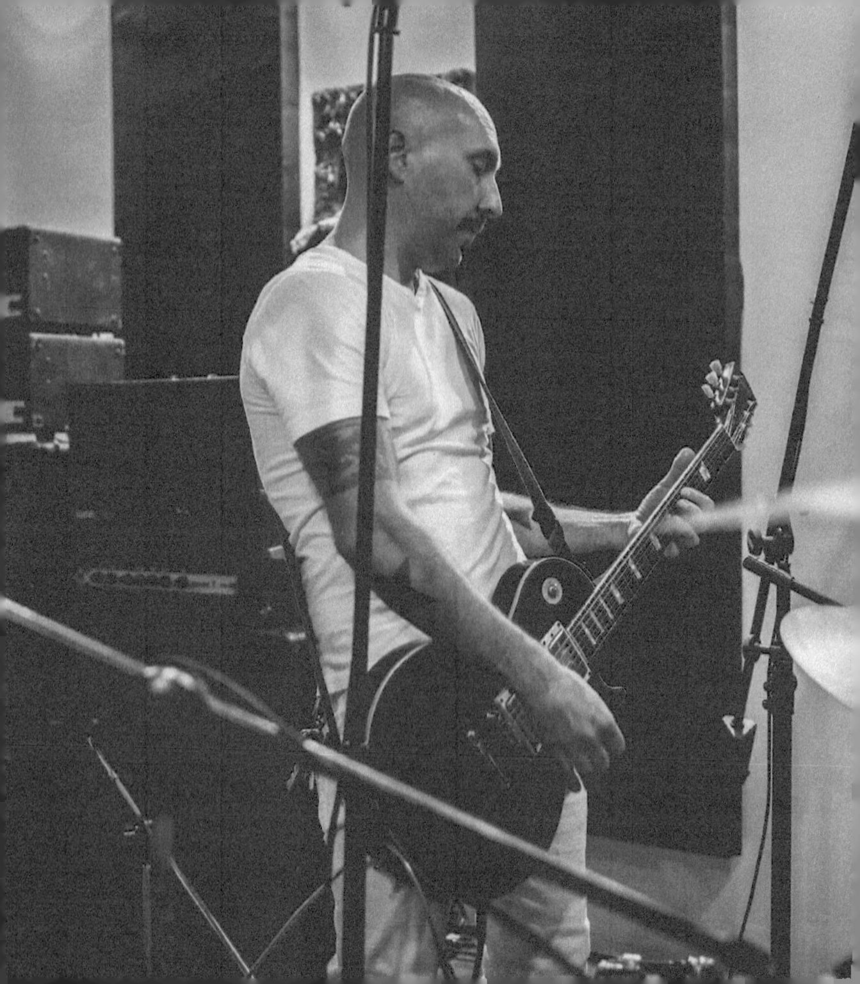

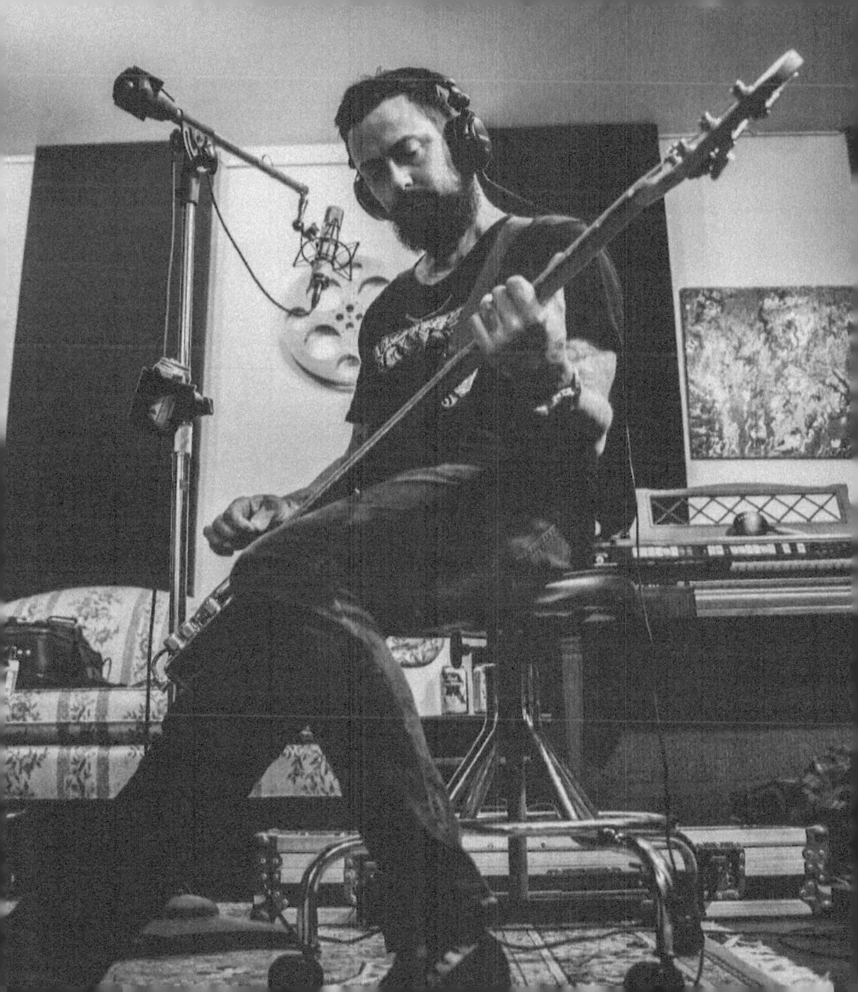

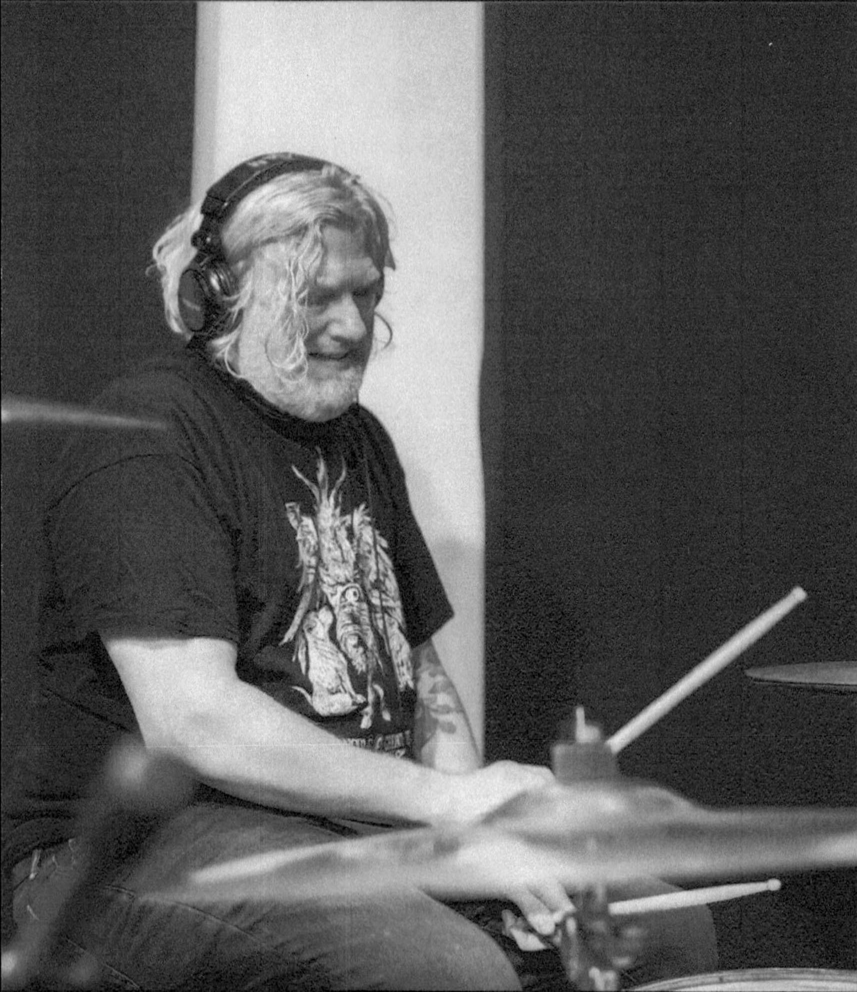

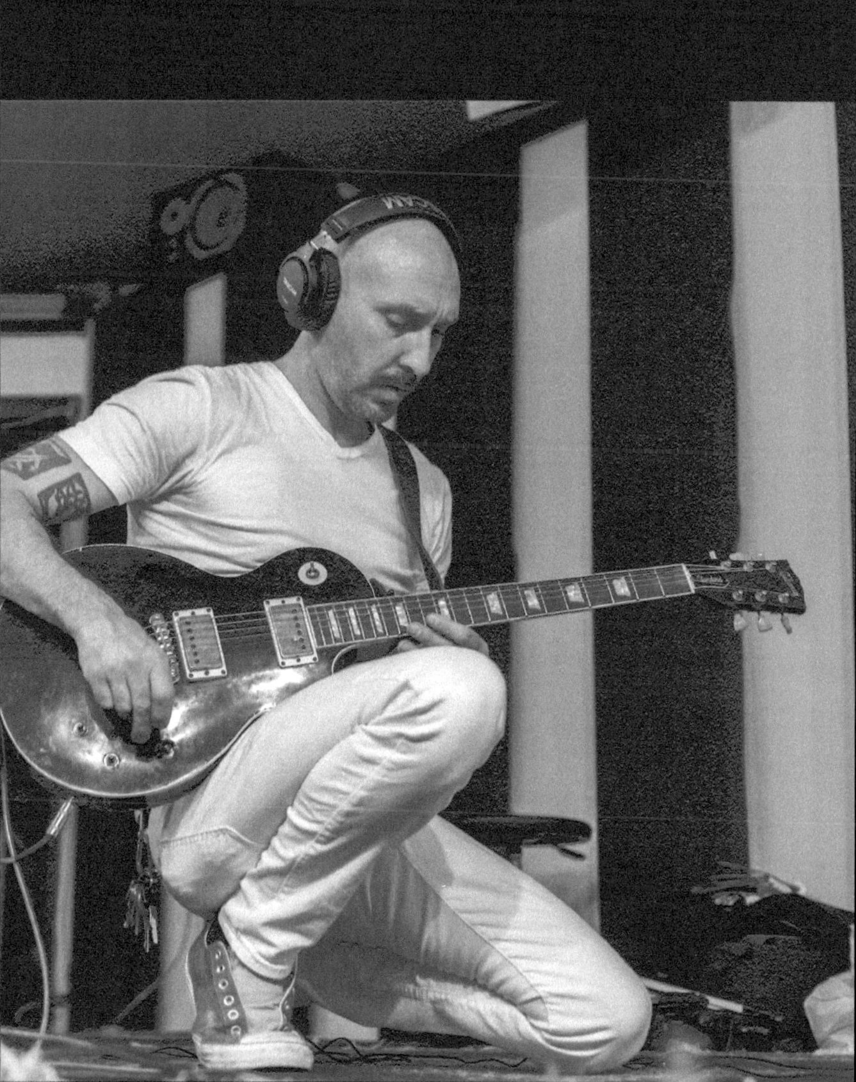

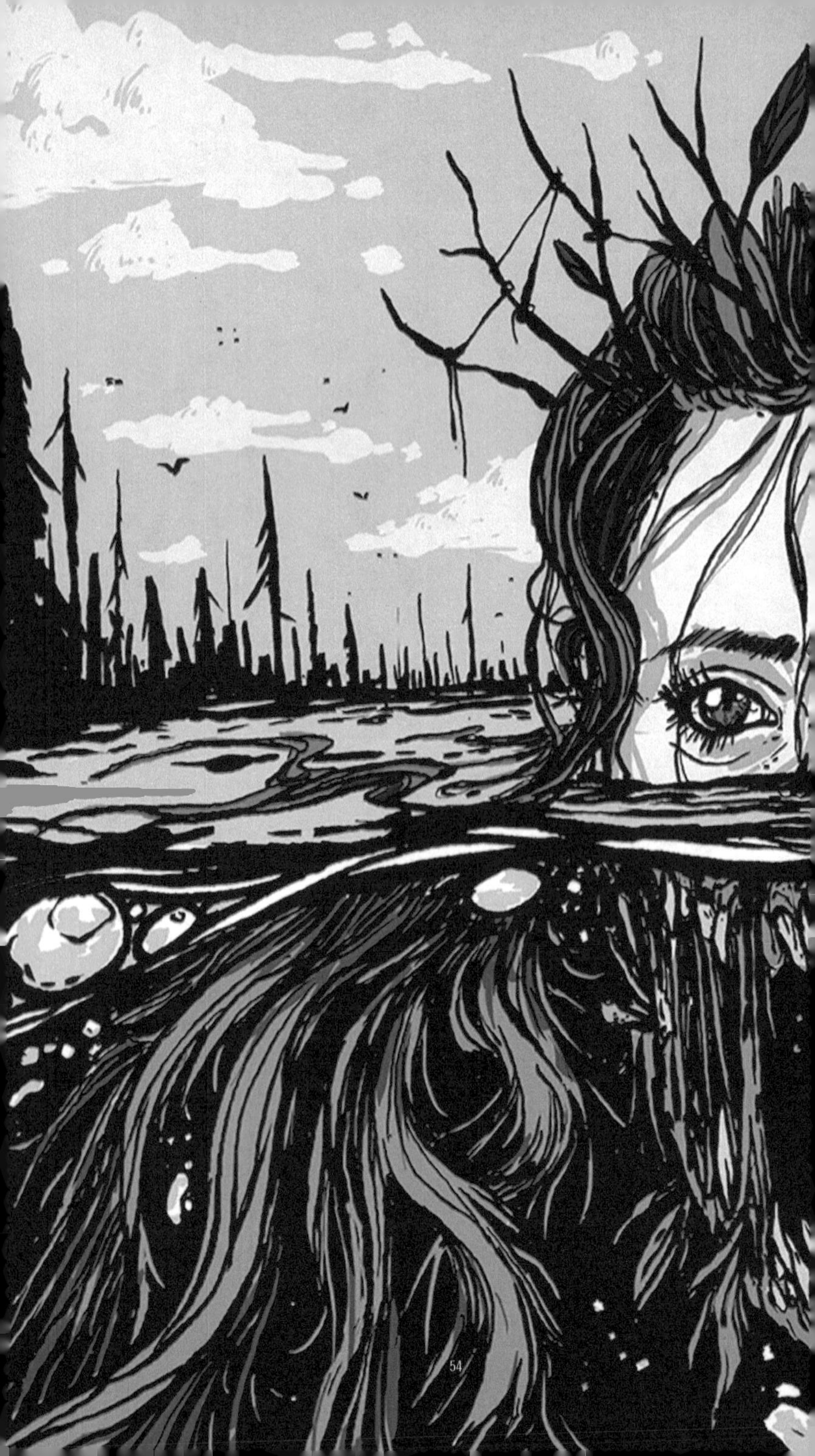

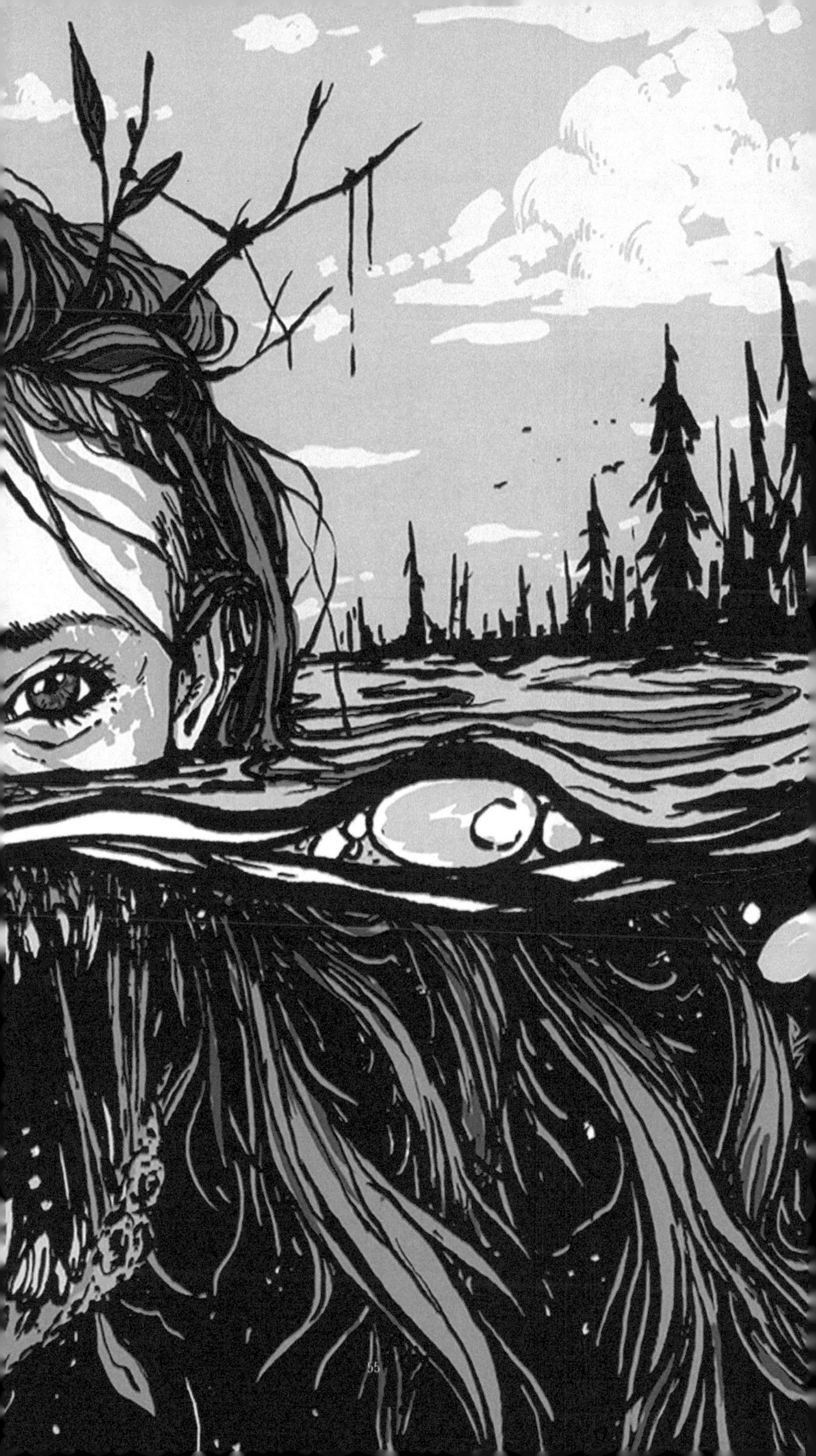

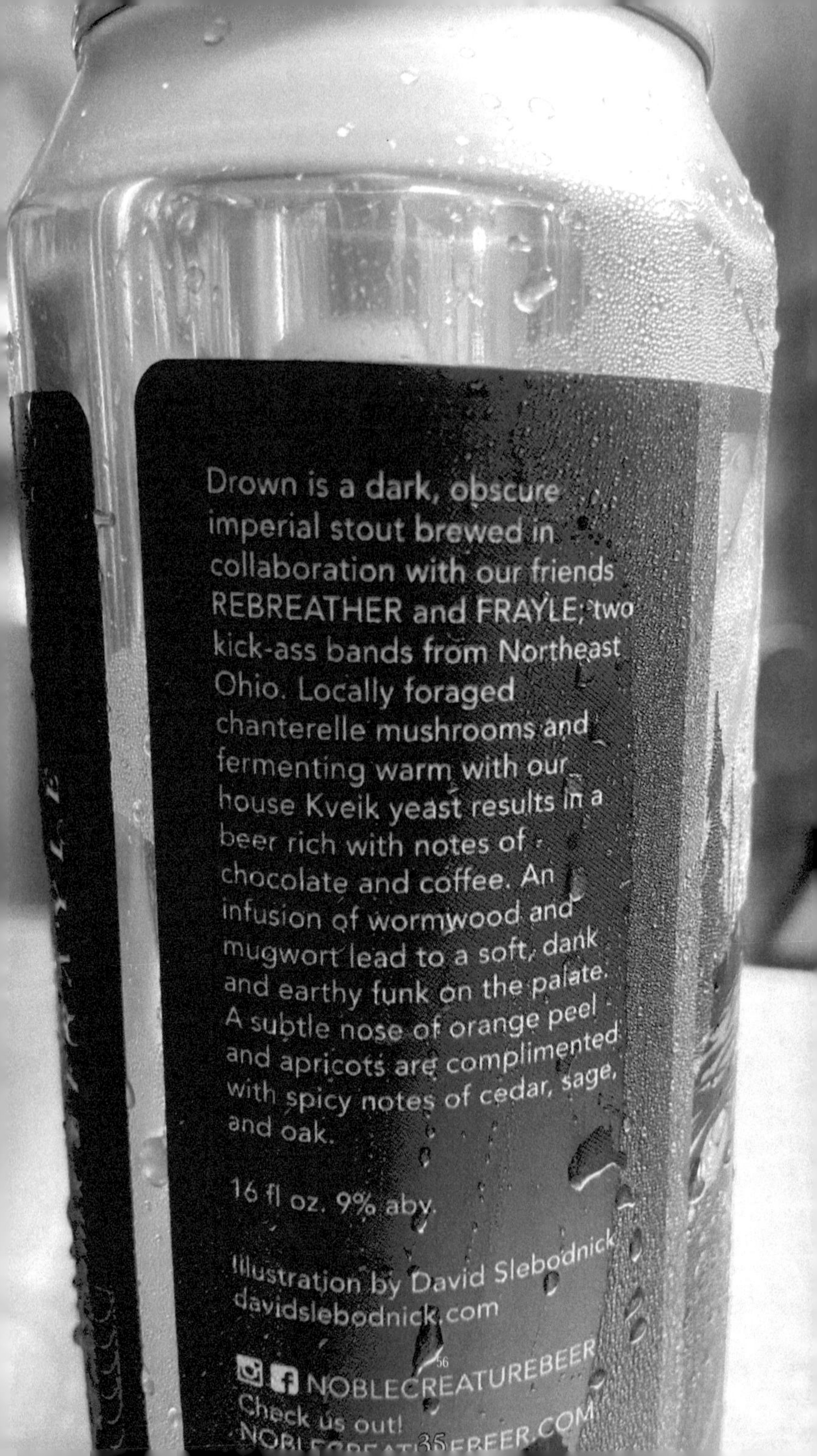

Drown is a dark, obscure imperial stout brewed in collaboration with our friends REBREATHER and FRAYLE; two kick-ass bands from Northeast Ohio. Locally foraged chanterelle mushrooms and fermenting warm with our house Kveik yeast results in a beer rich with notes of chocolate and coffee. An infusion of wormwood and mugwort lead to a soft, dank and earthy funk on the palate. A subtle nose of orange peel and apricots are complimented with spicy notes of cedar, sage, and oak.

16 fl oz. 9% abv.

Illustration by David Slebodnick
davidslebodnick.com

NOBLECREATUREBEER
Check us out!
NOBLECREATUREBEER.COM

DROWN

We collaborated with our friends FRAYLE for this song and video, then partnered with the amazing crew at Noble Creature Cask House here in Youngstown, Ohio on a beer to release along with the single. We had a great time creating this and cannot thank everyone involved enough for all your hard work.

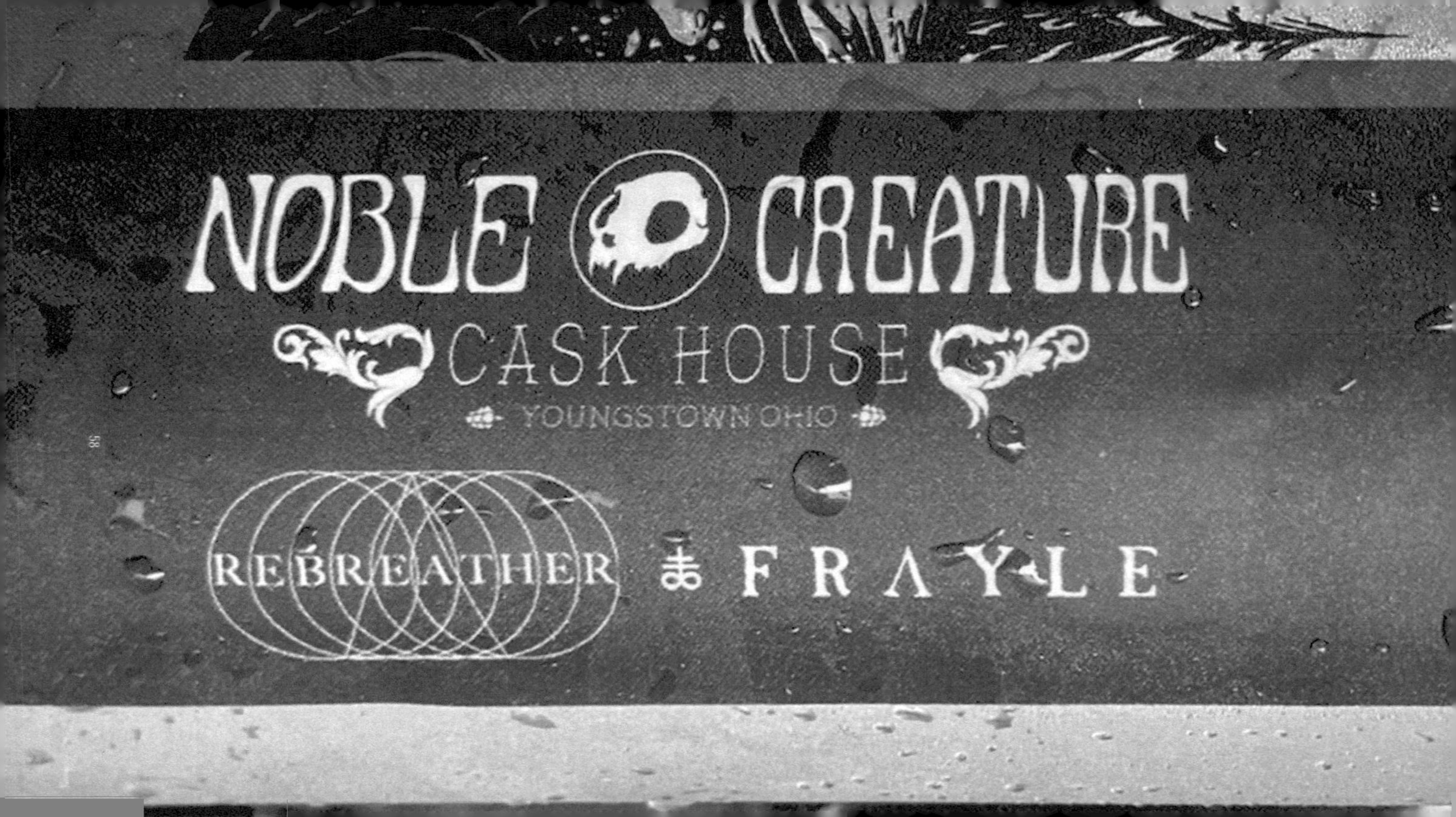

NOBLE CREATURE
CASK HOUSE
YOUNGSTOWN OHIO

REBREATHER

FRAYLE

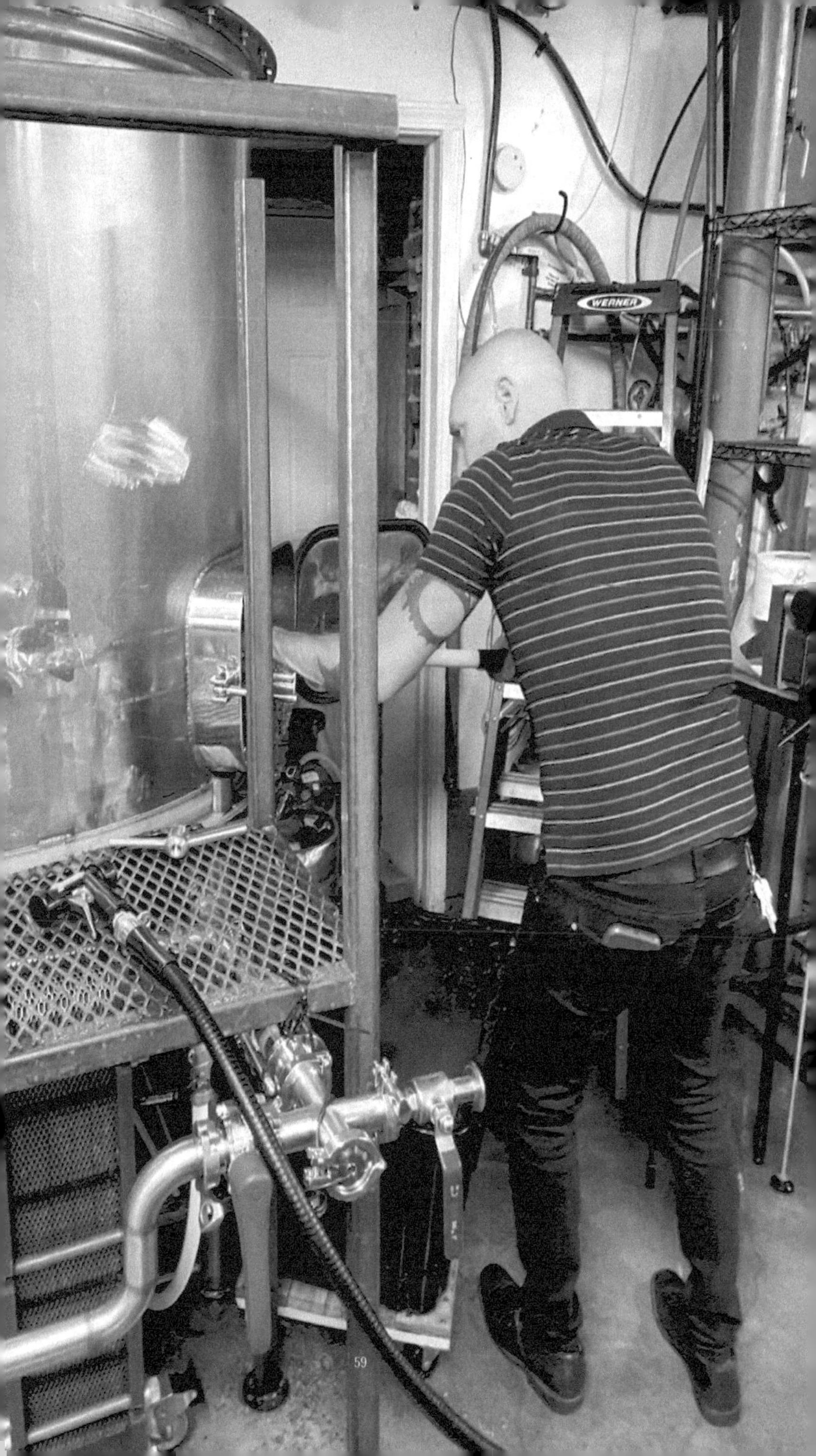
WERNER

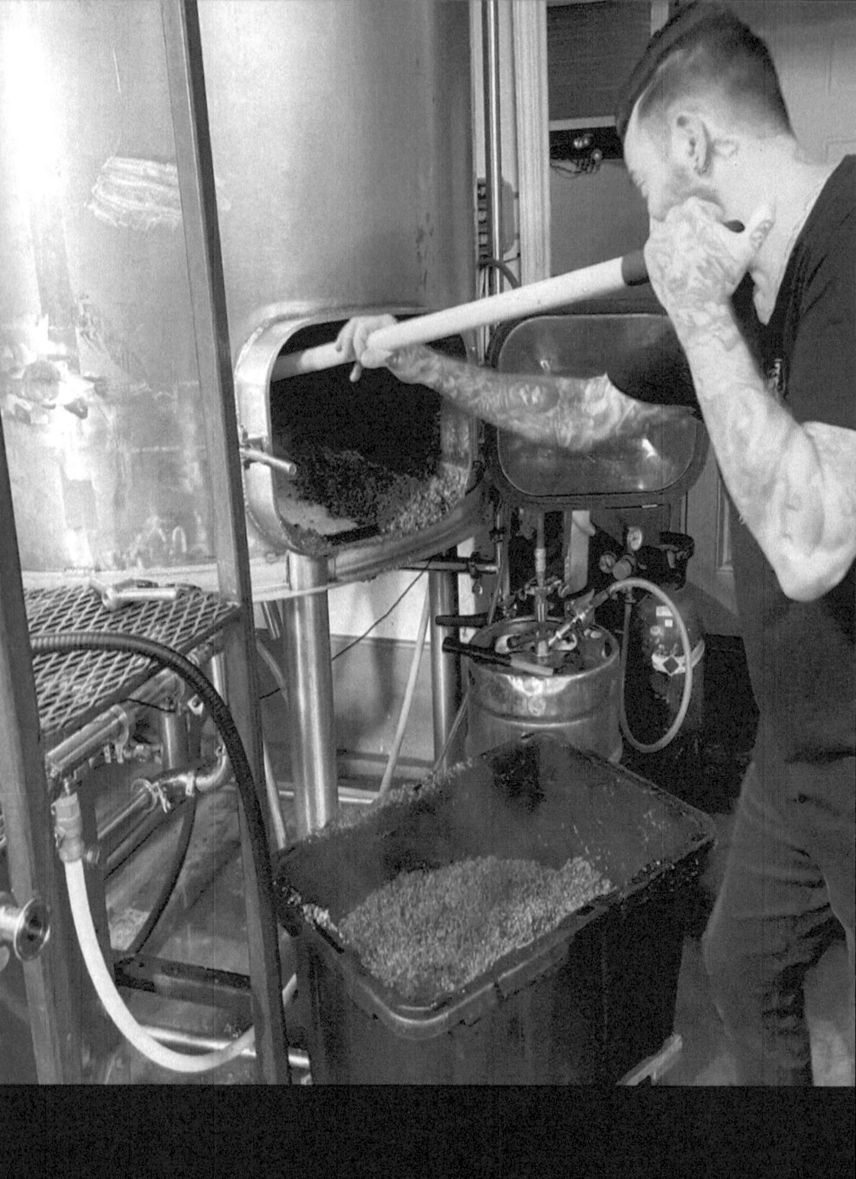

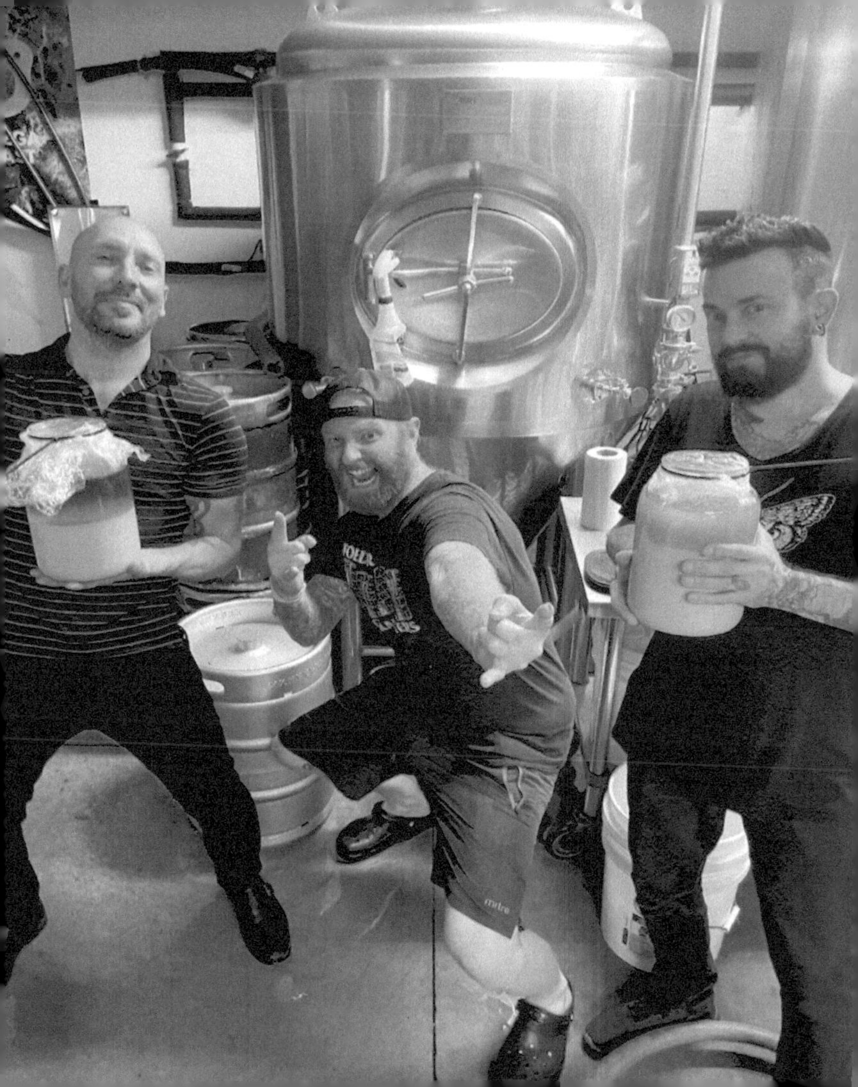

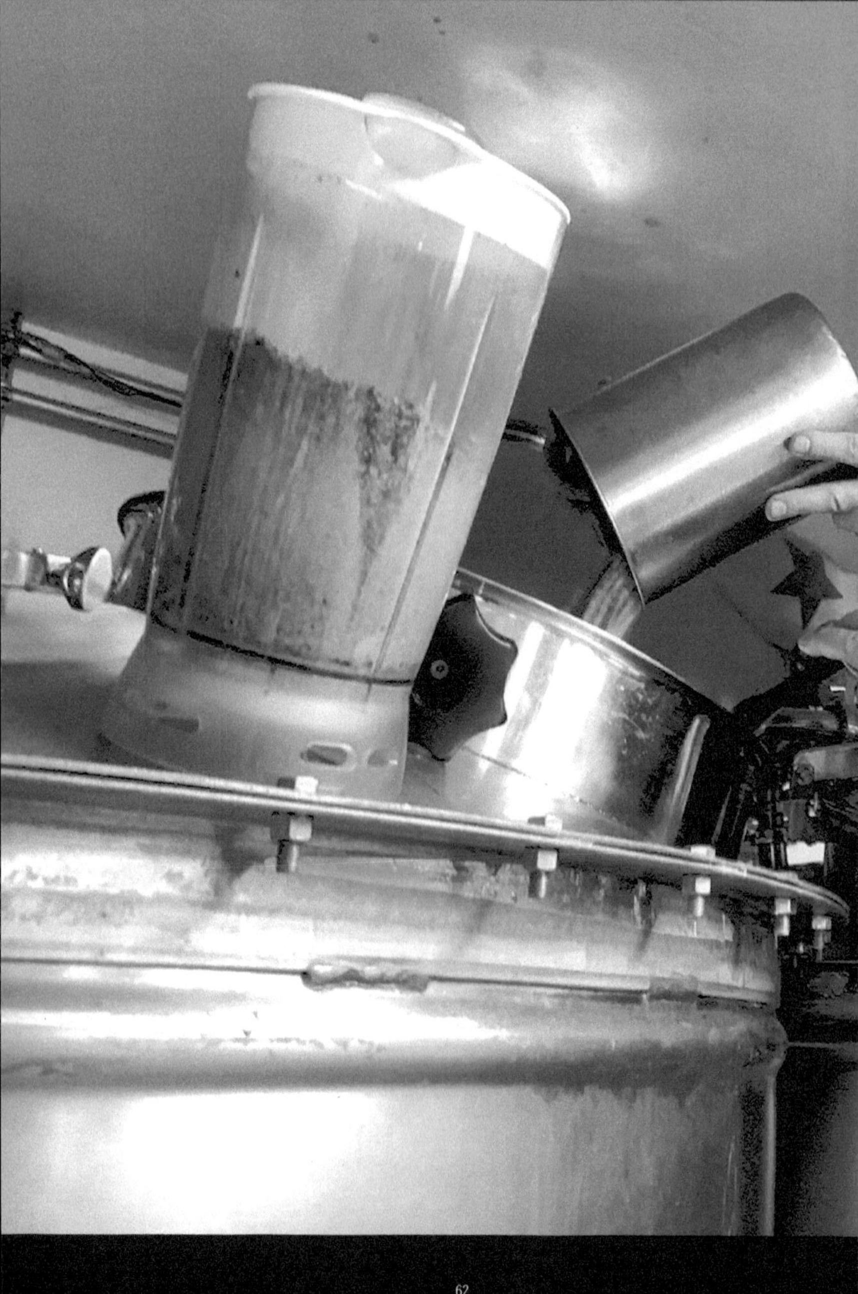

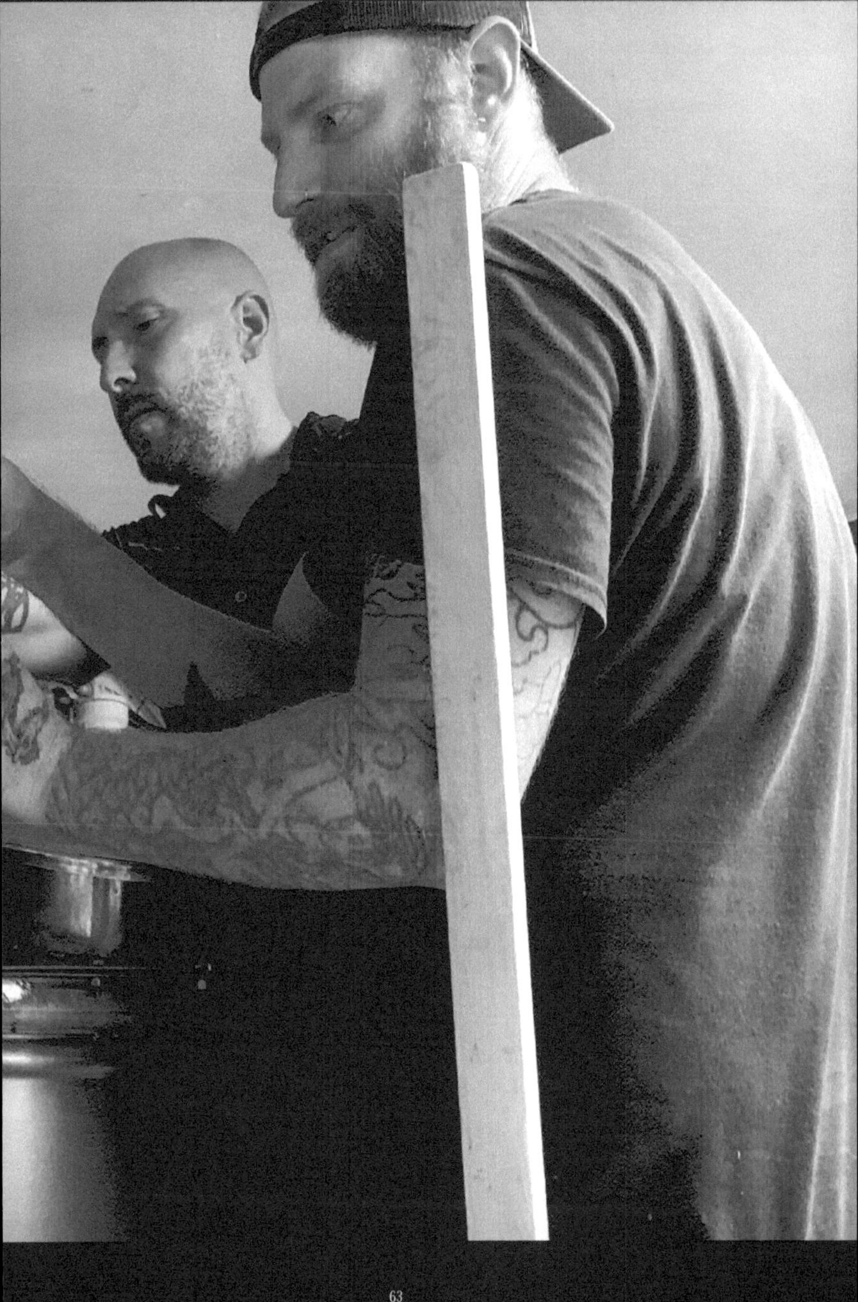

NOBLE CREATURE
CASK HOUSE
REBREATHER
#8 FRAYLE

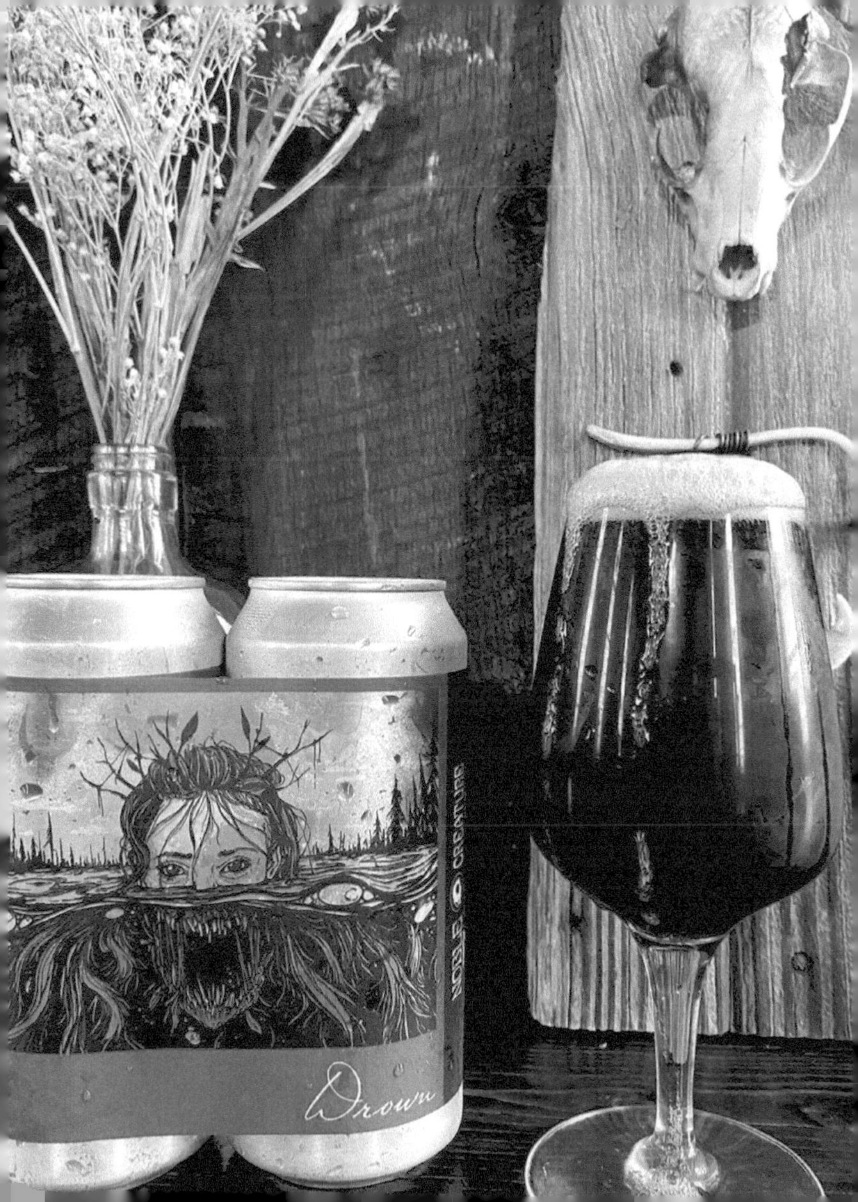
NOBLE CREATURES
Drown

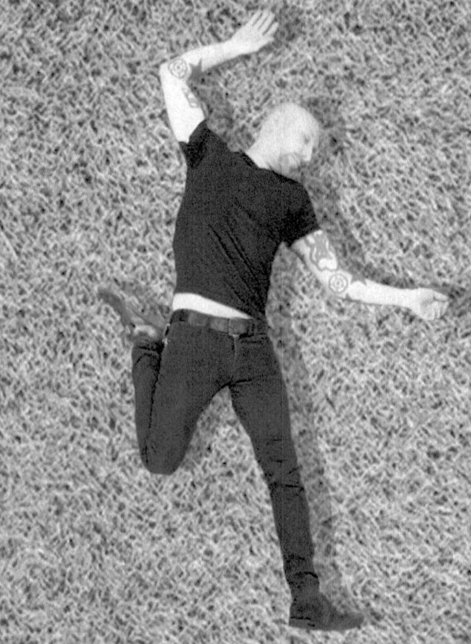

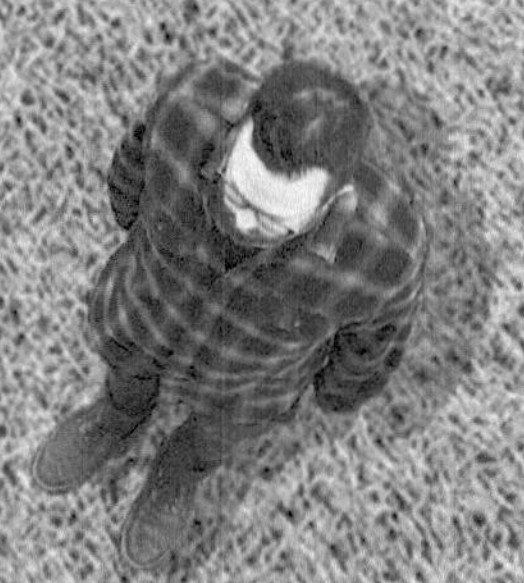

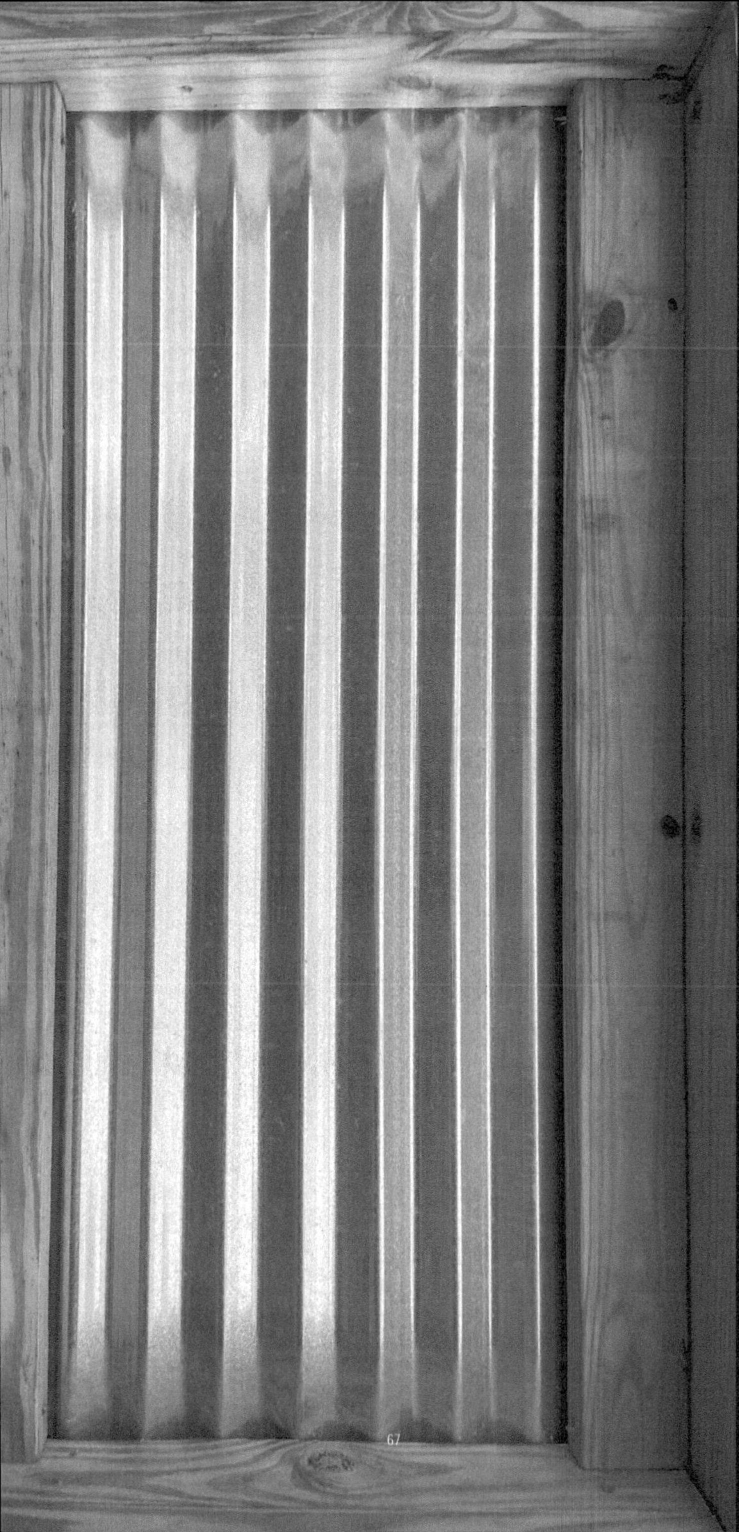

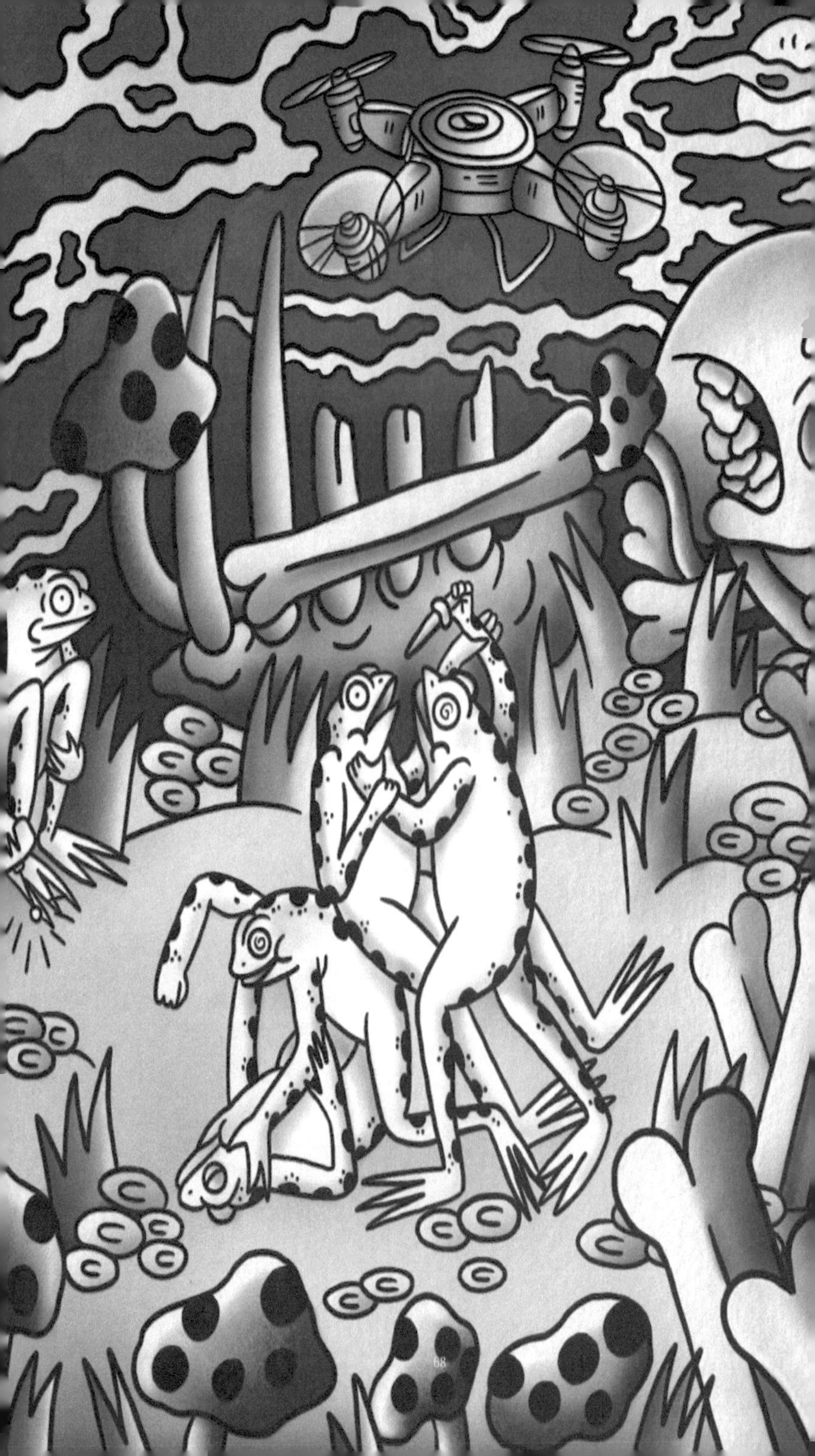

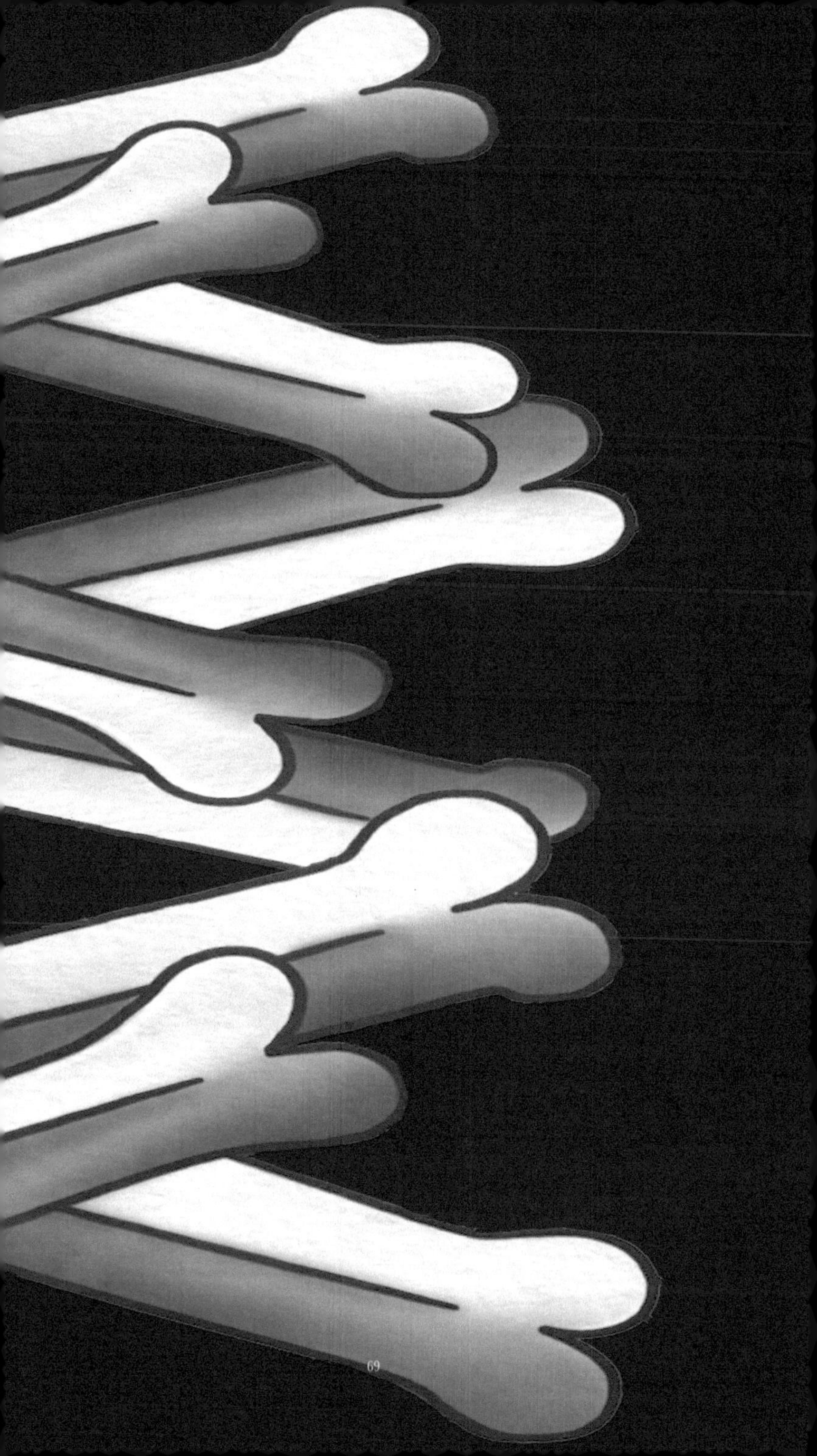

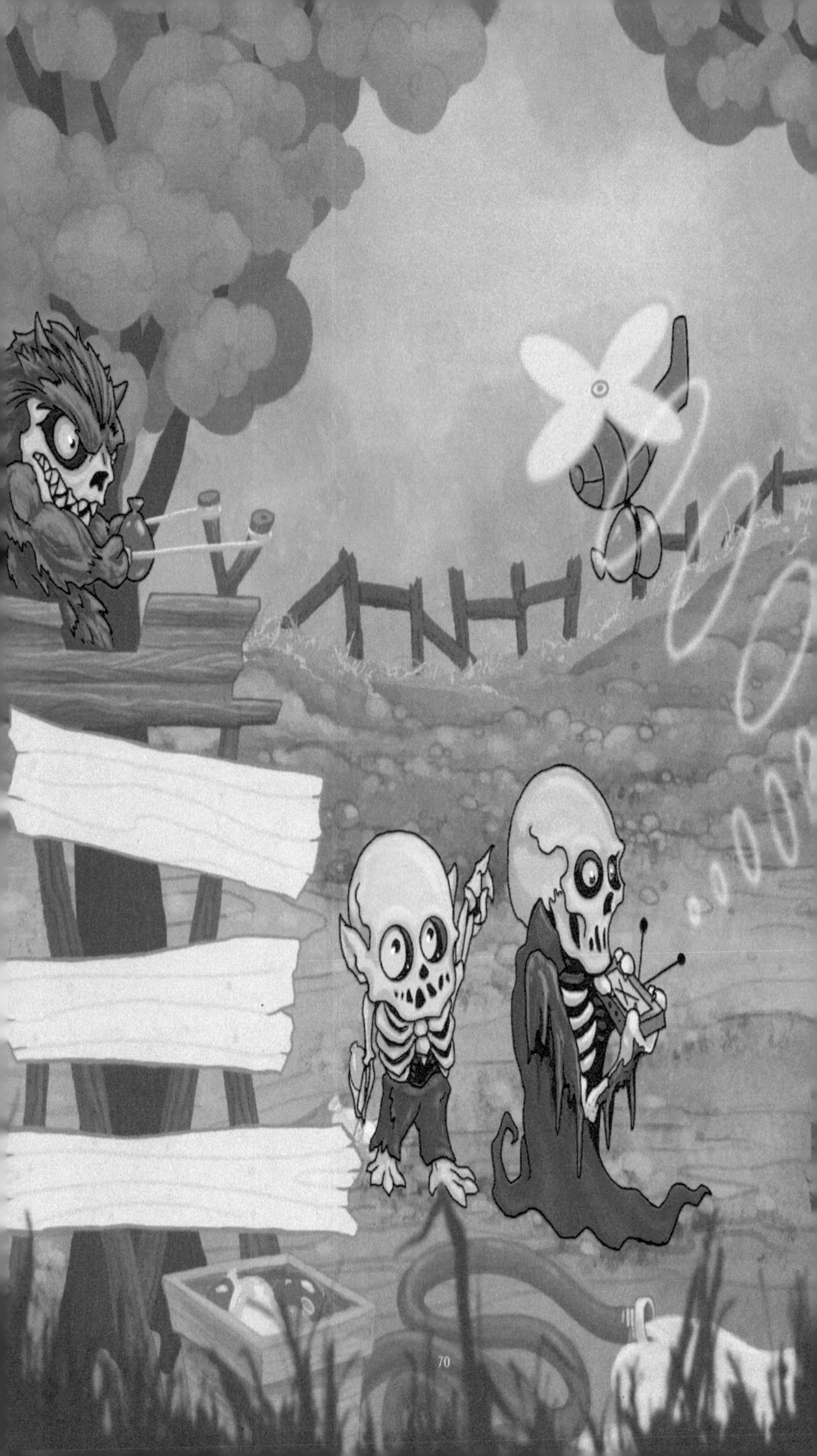

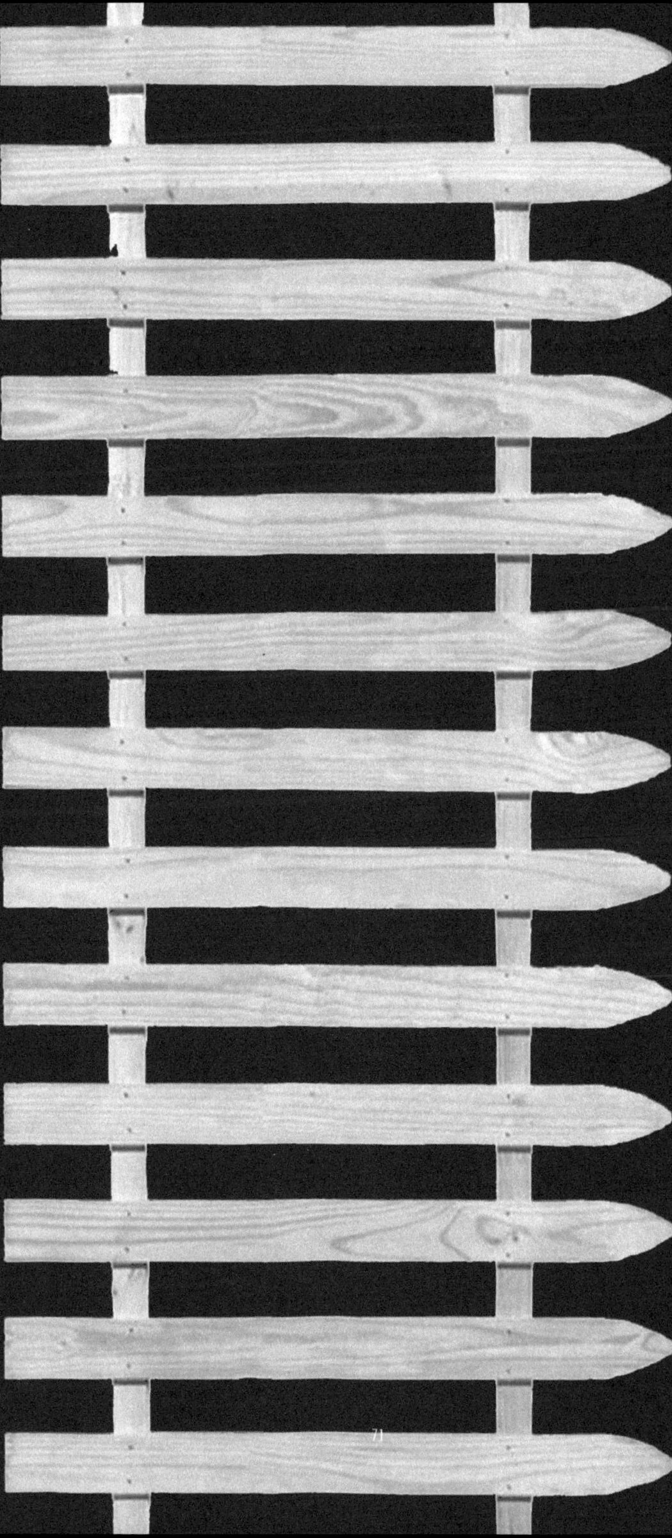

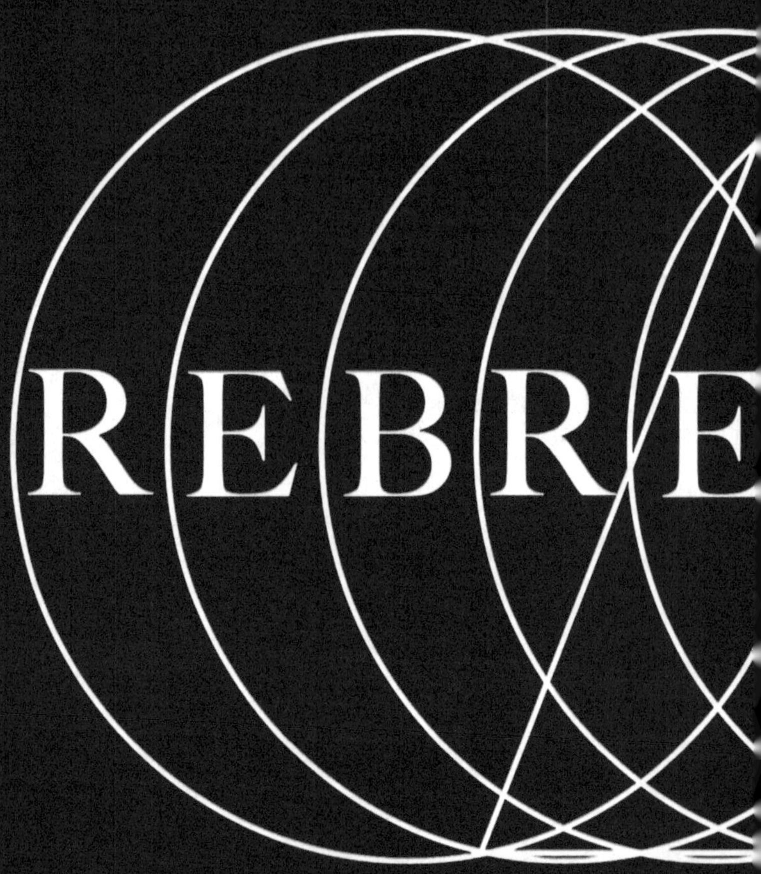
REBRE

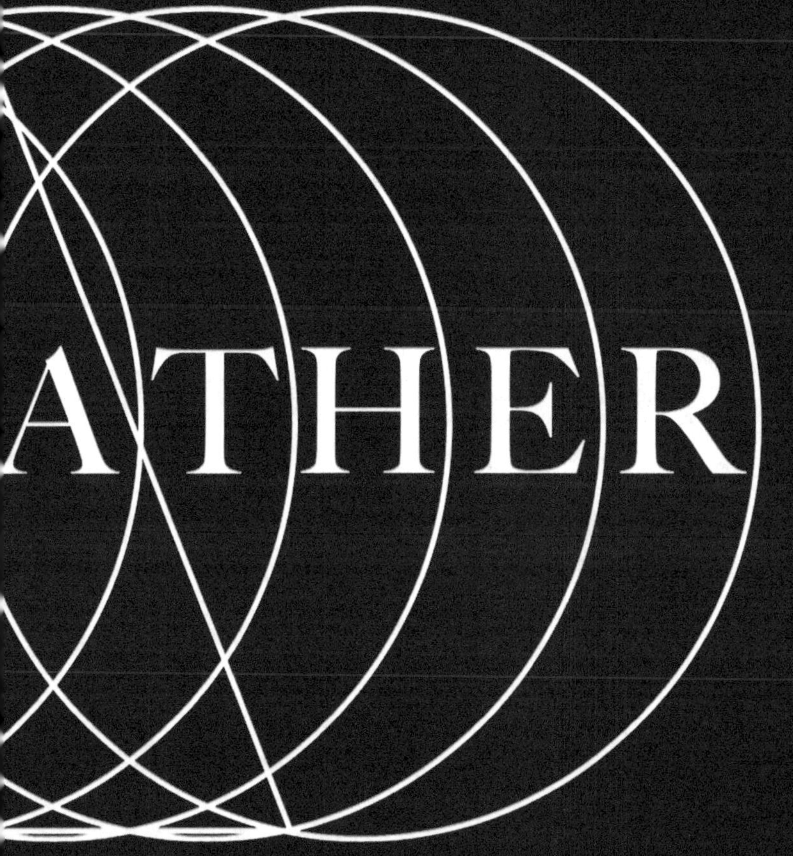
ATHER

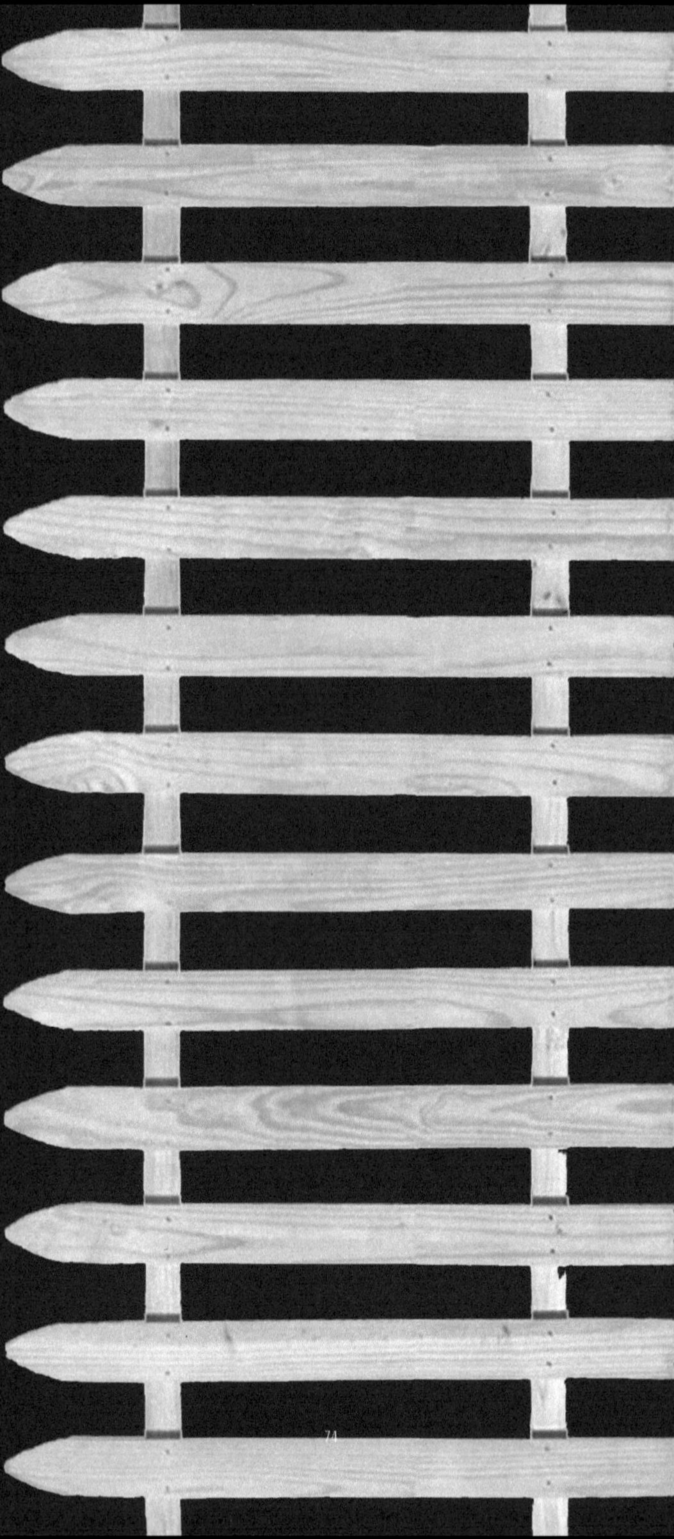

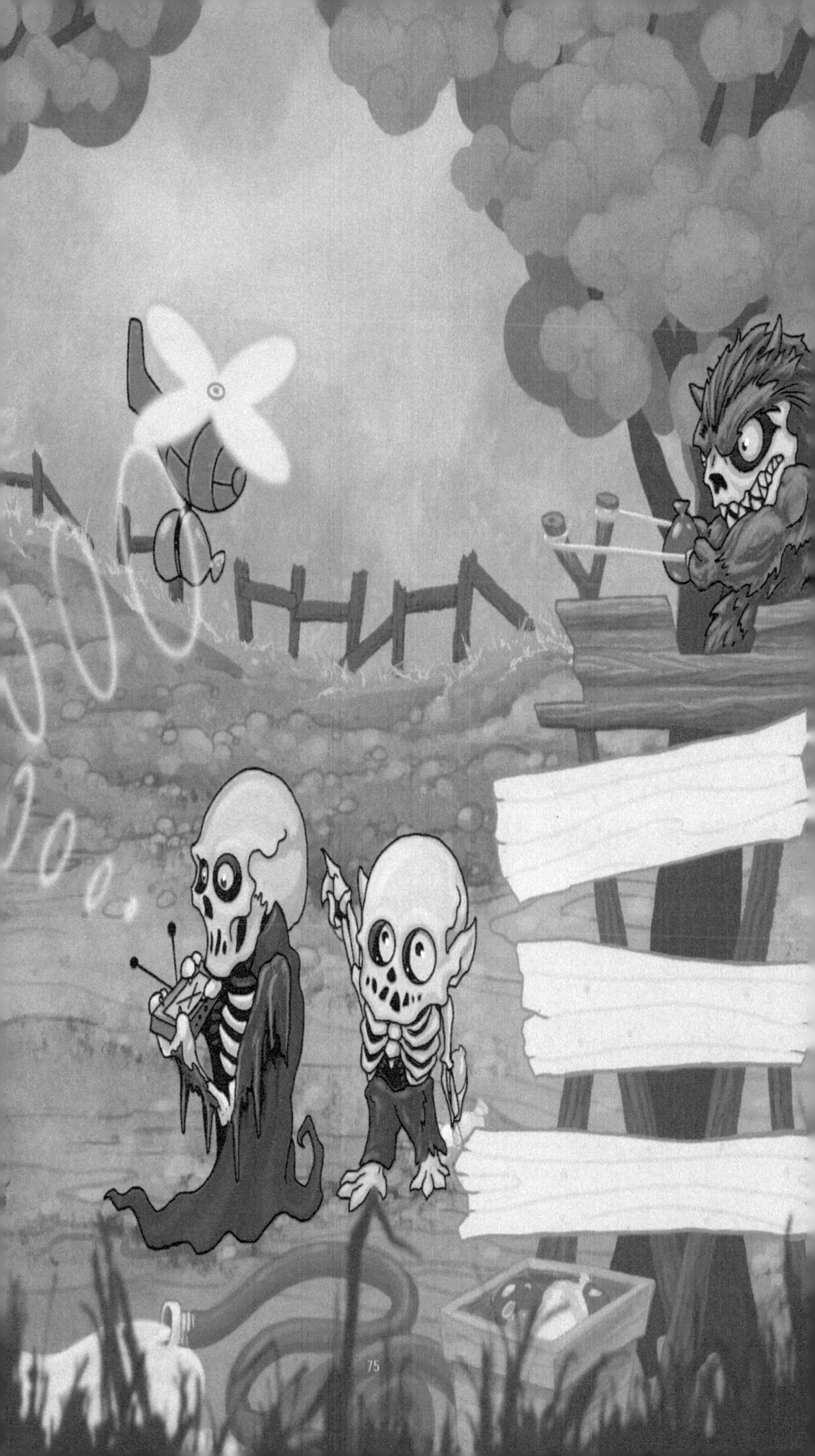

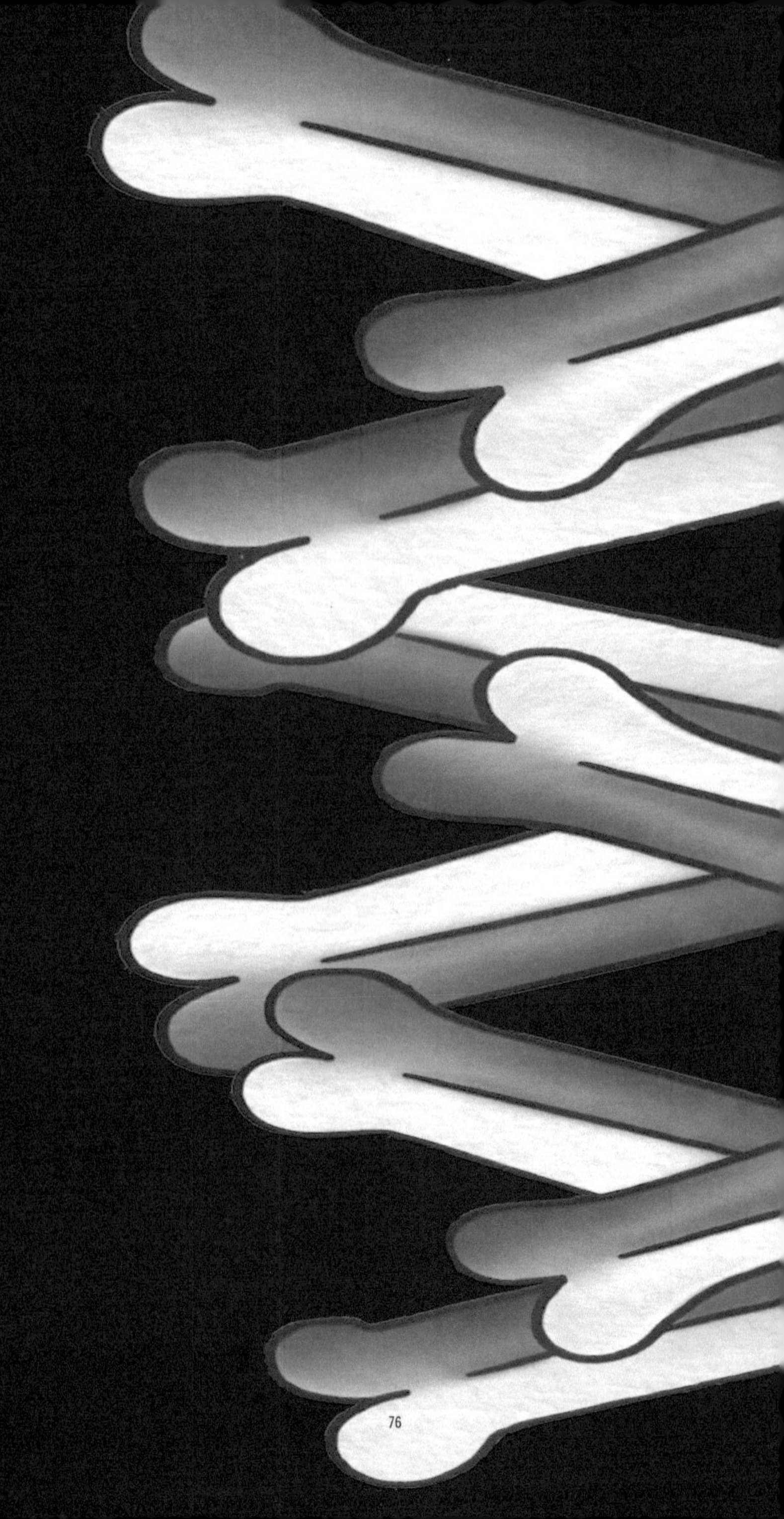

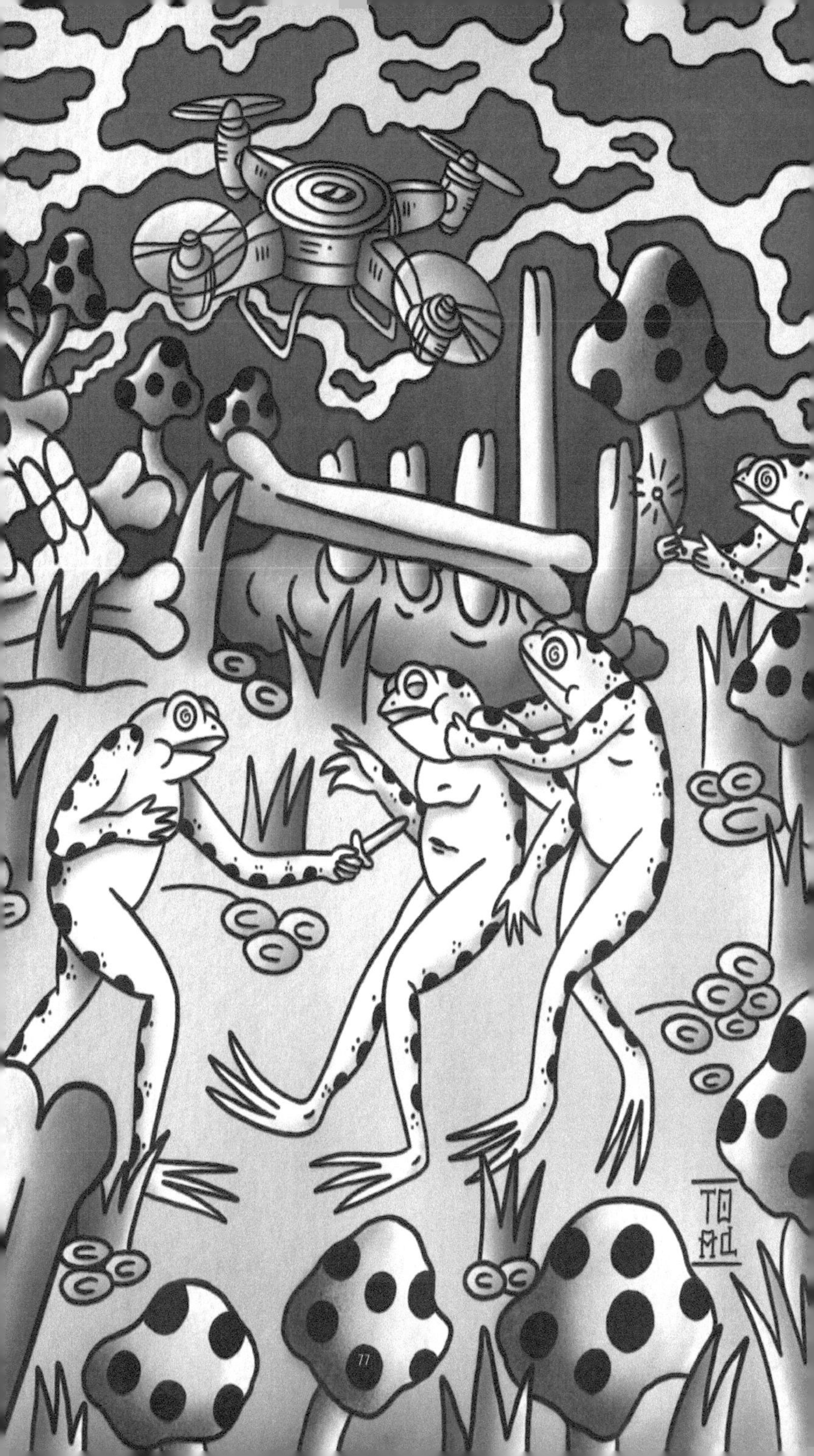
TO
Md

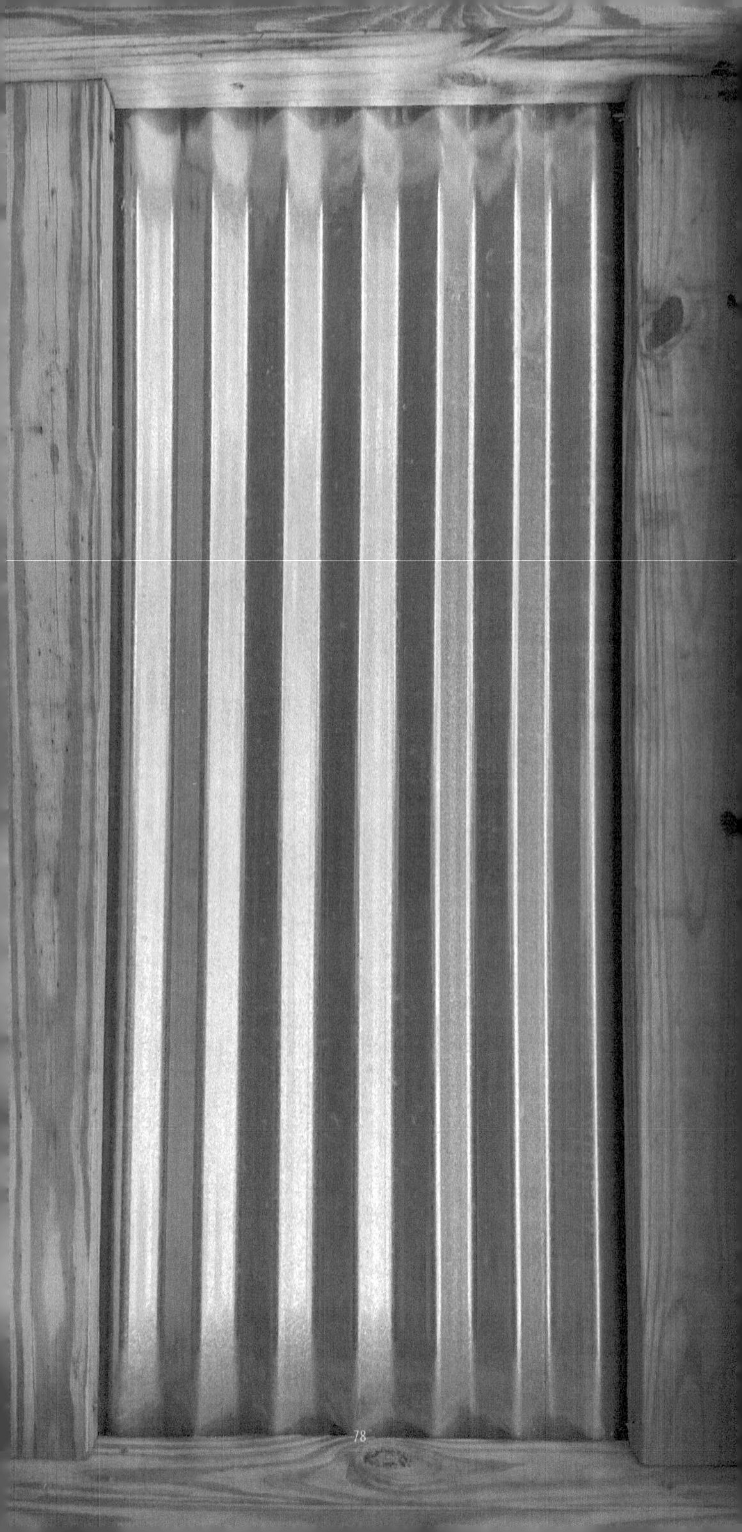

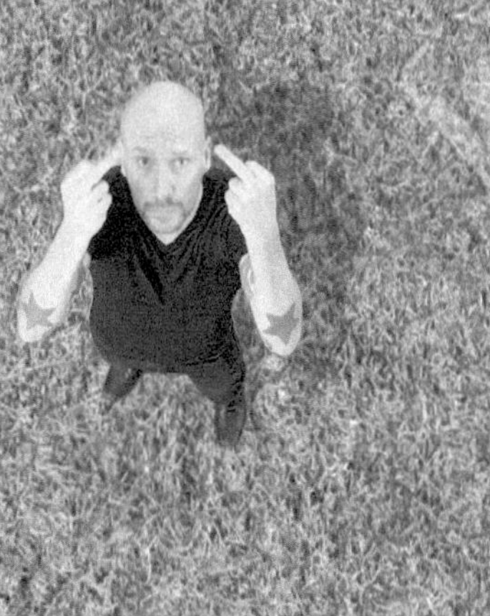

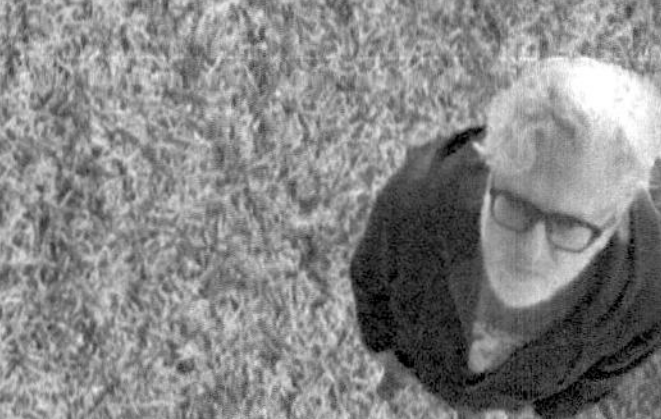

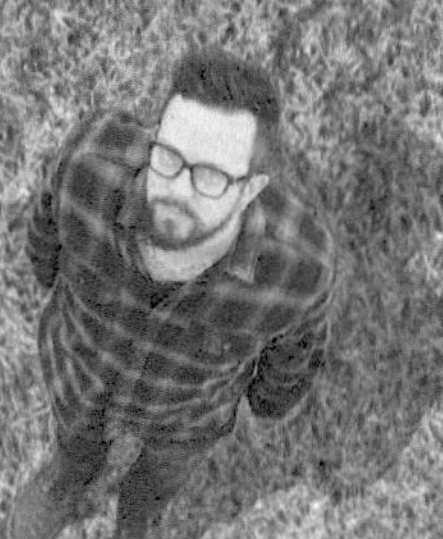

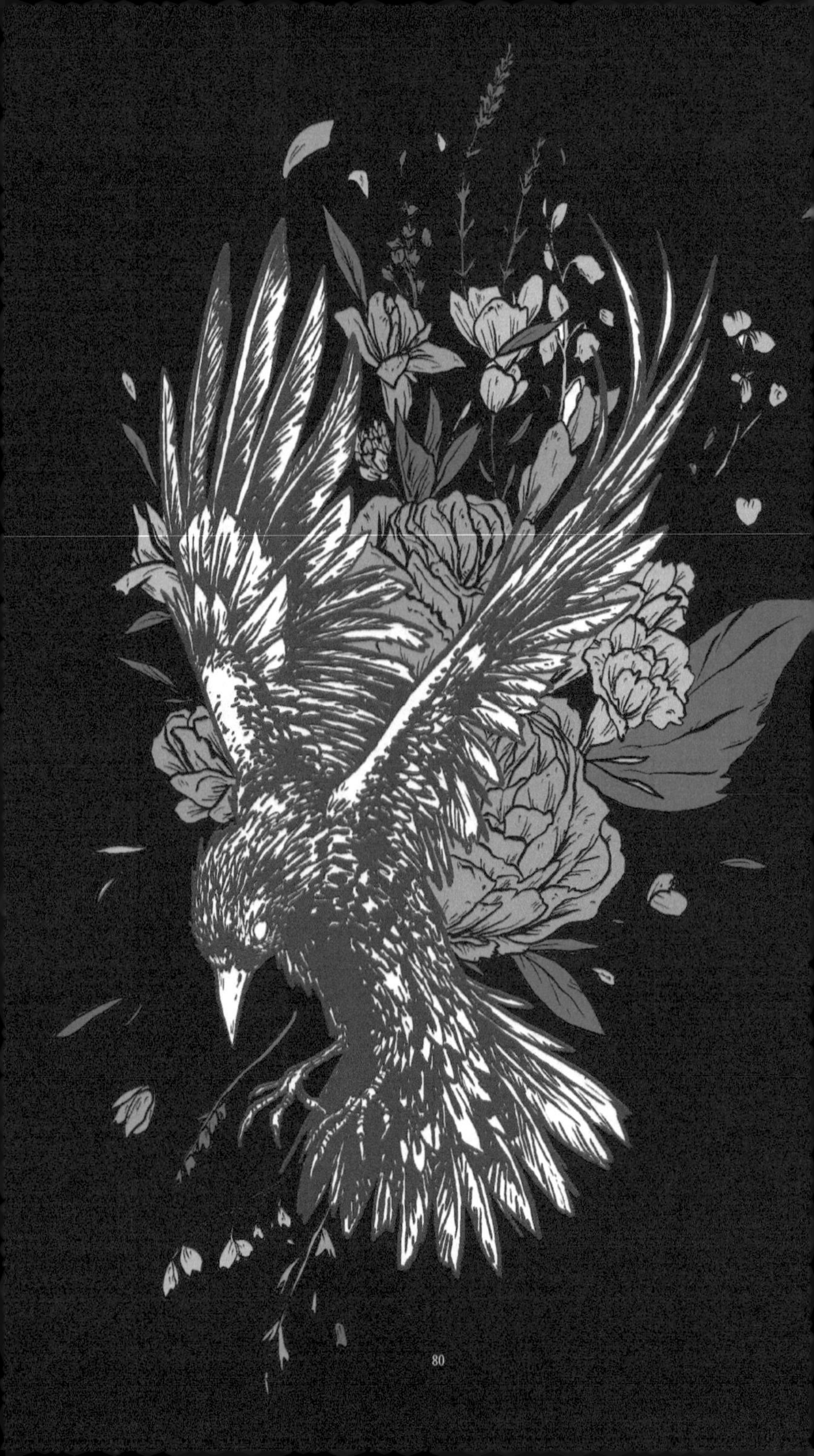

LITTLE BLACKBIRD PHOTO

The talented Mollie Crowe of LITTLE BLACKBIRD PHOTO has captured us many times in many places over the last few years. These are just a small sample of her amazing work.

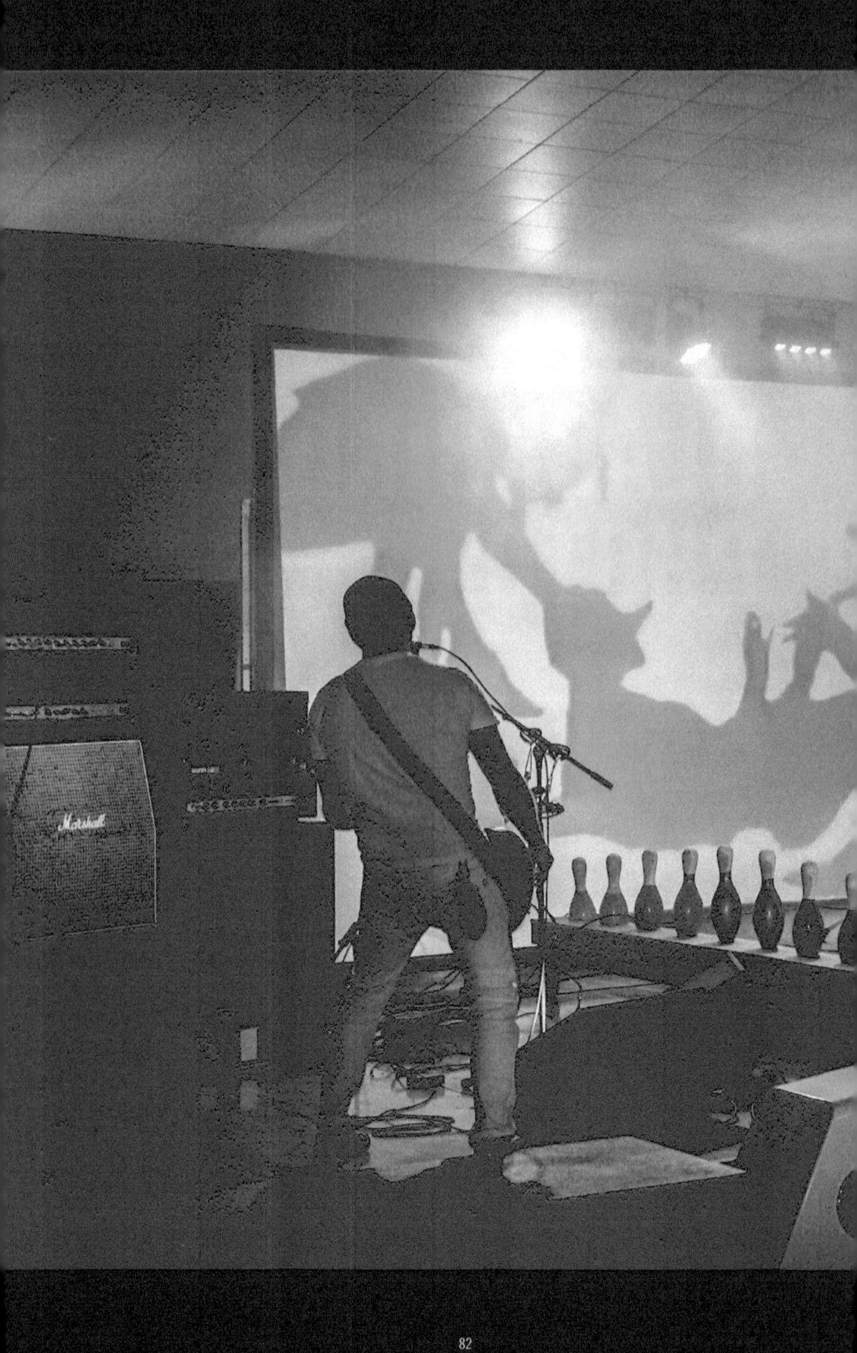
Marshall

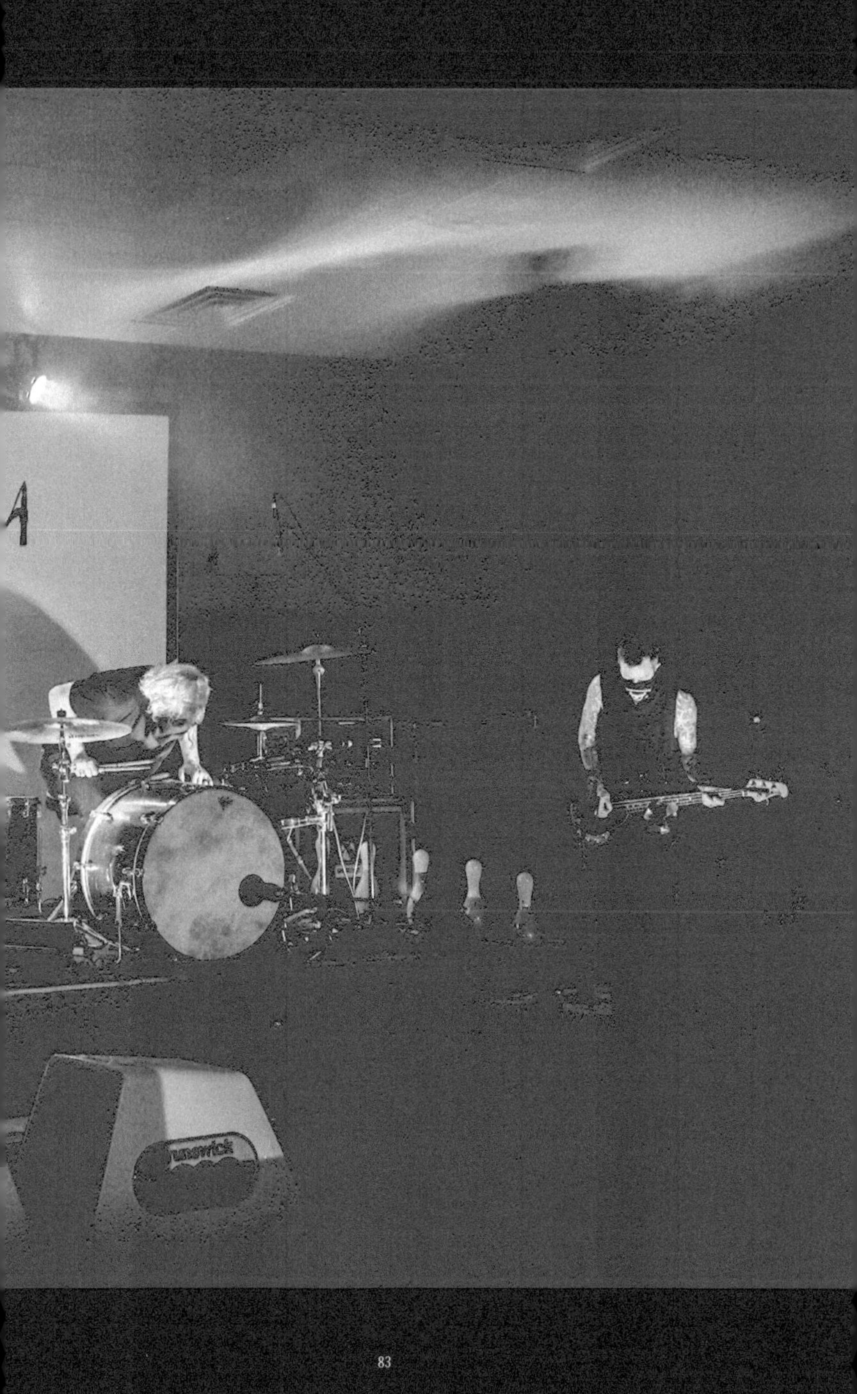

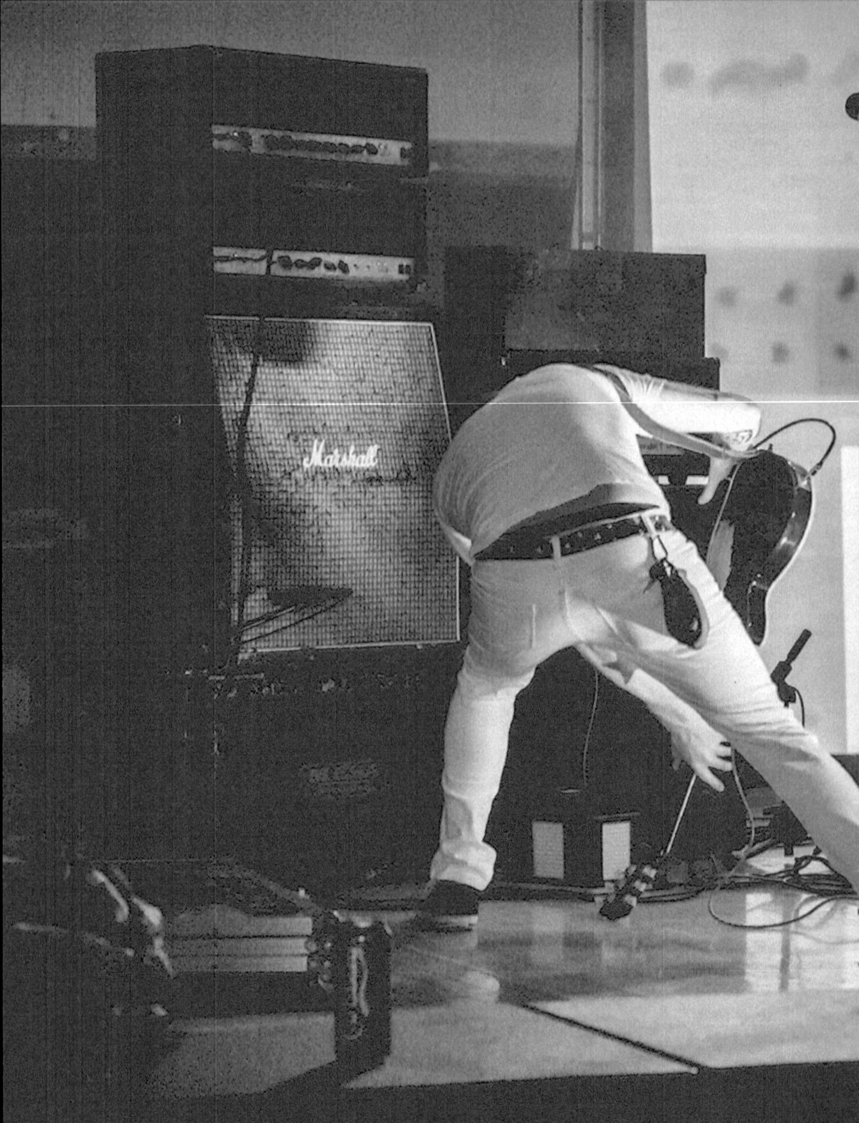
Marshall

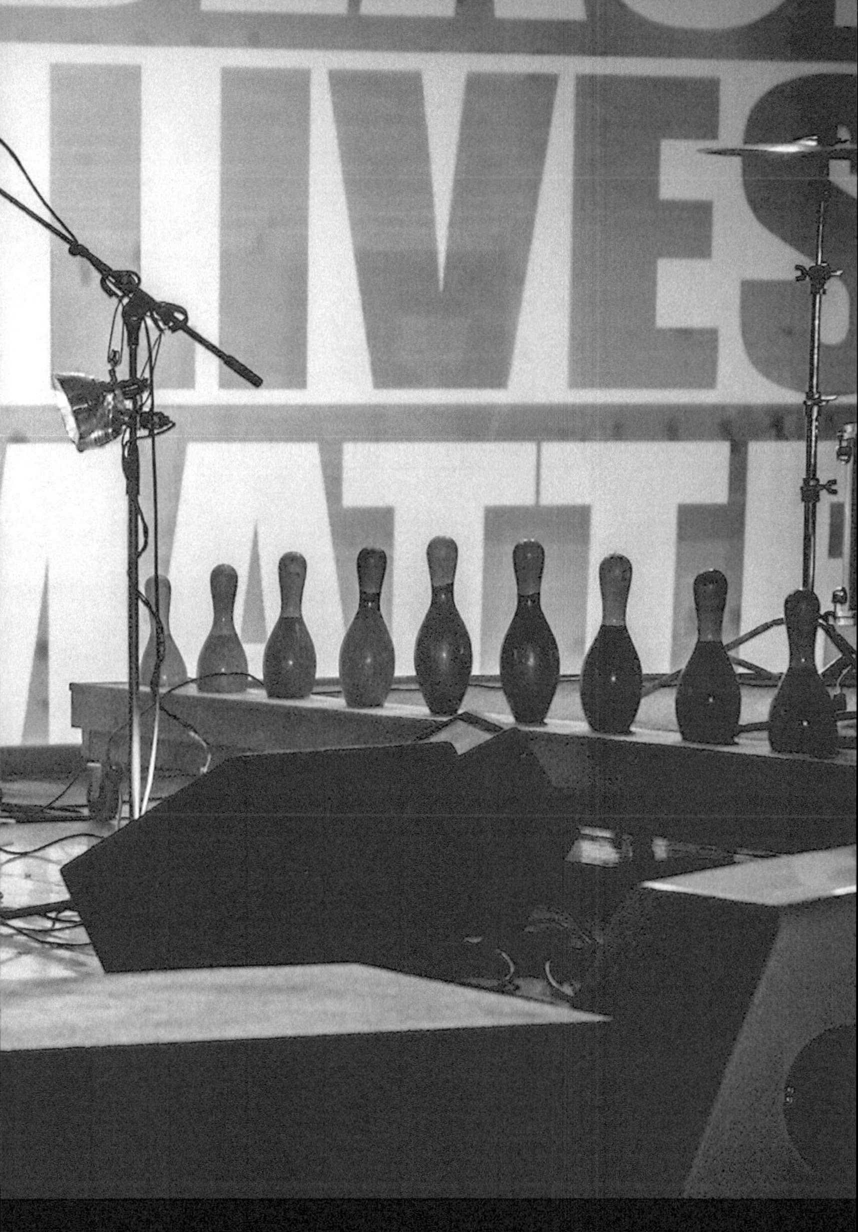

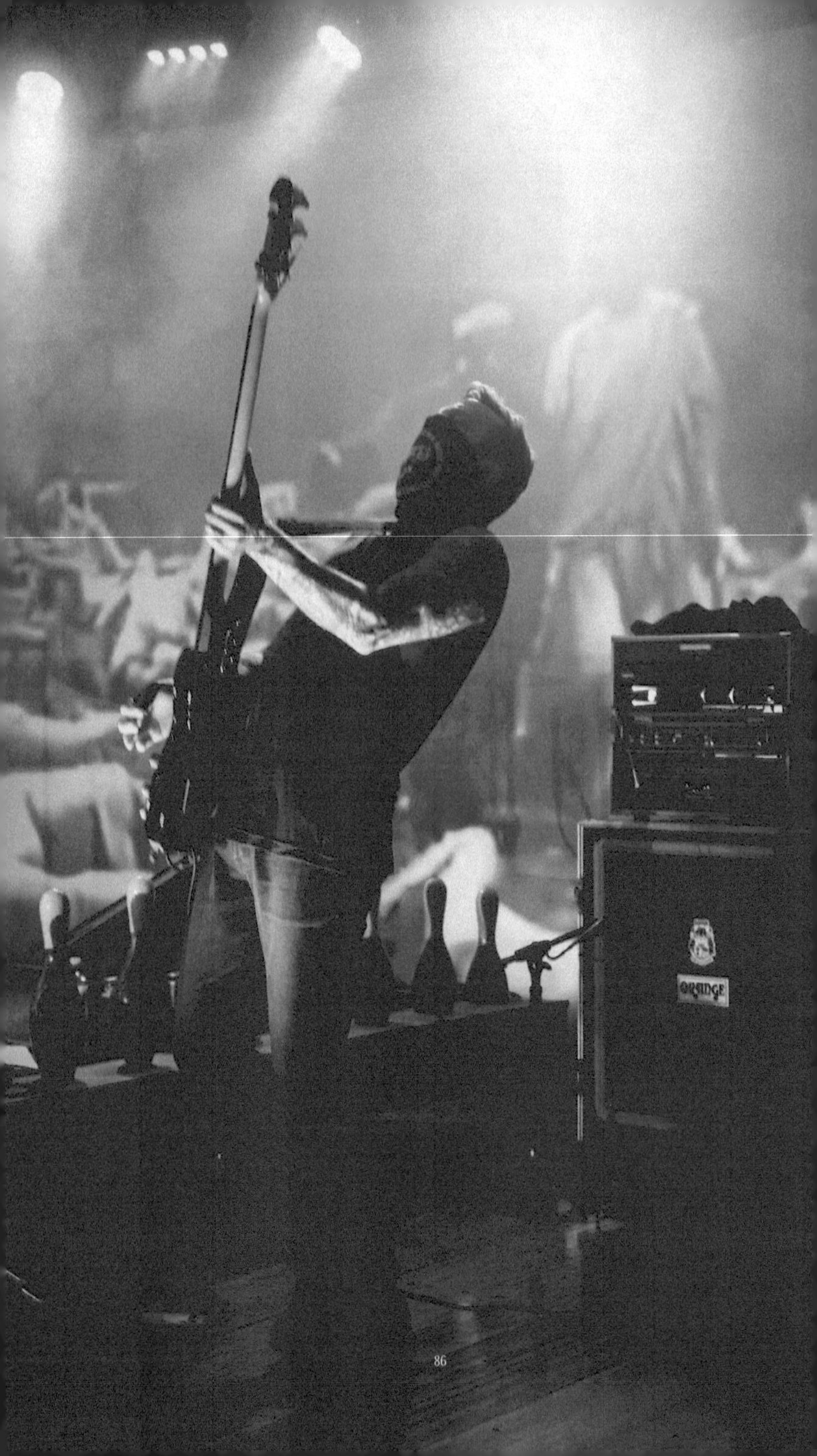
ORANGE

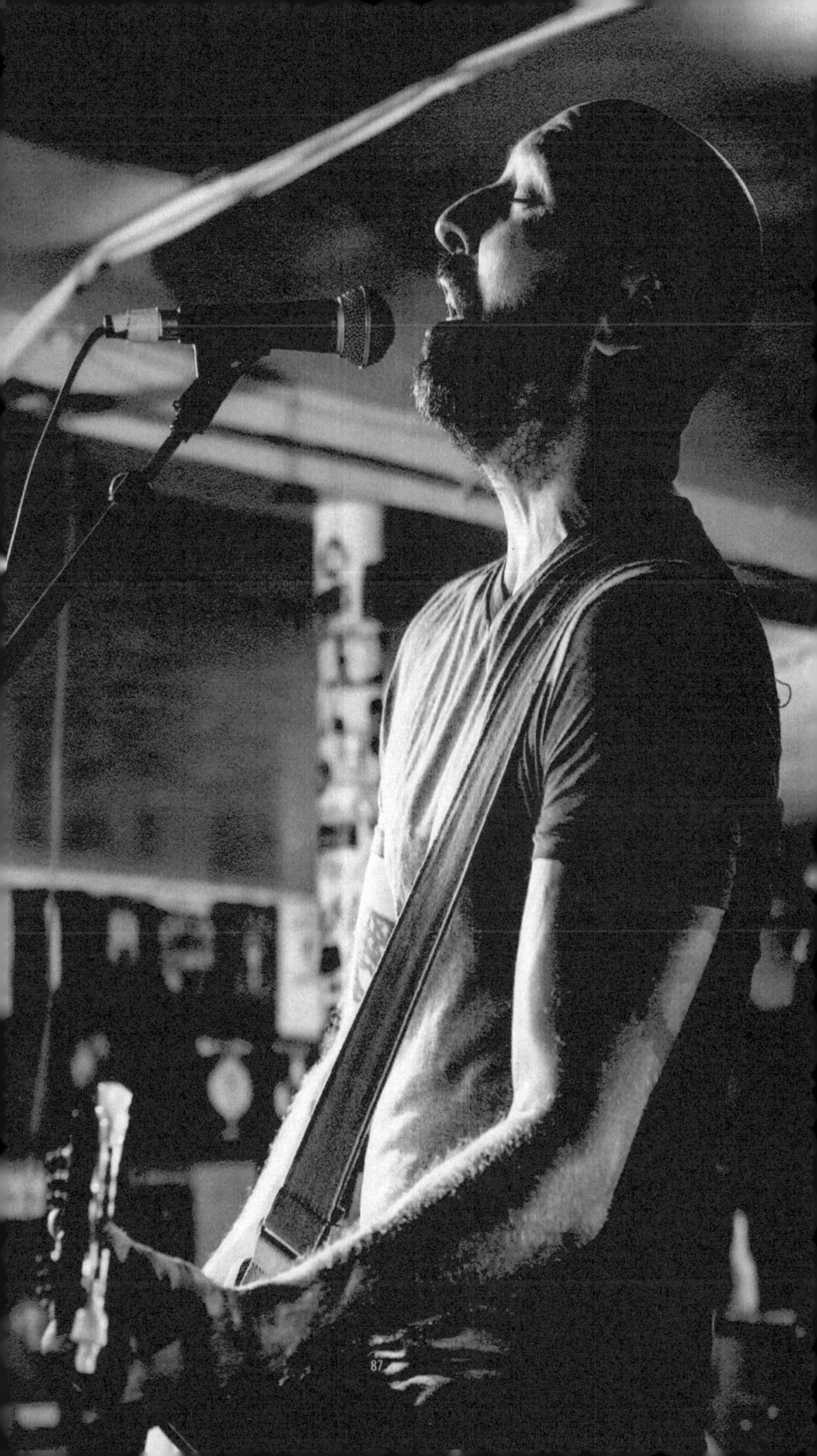

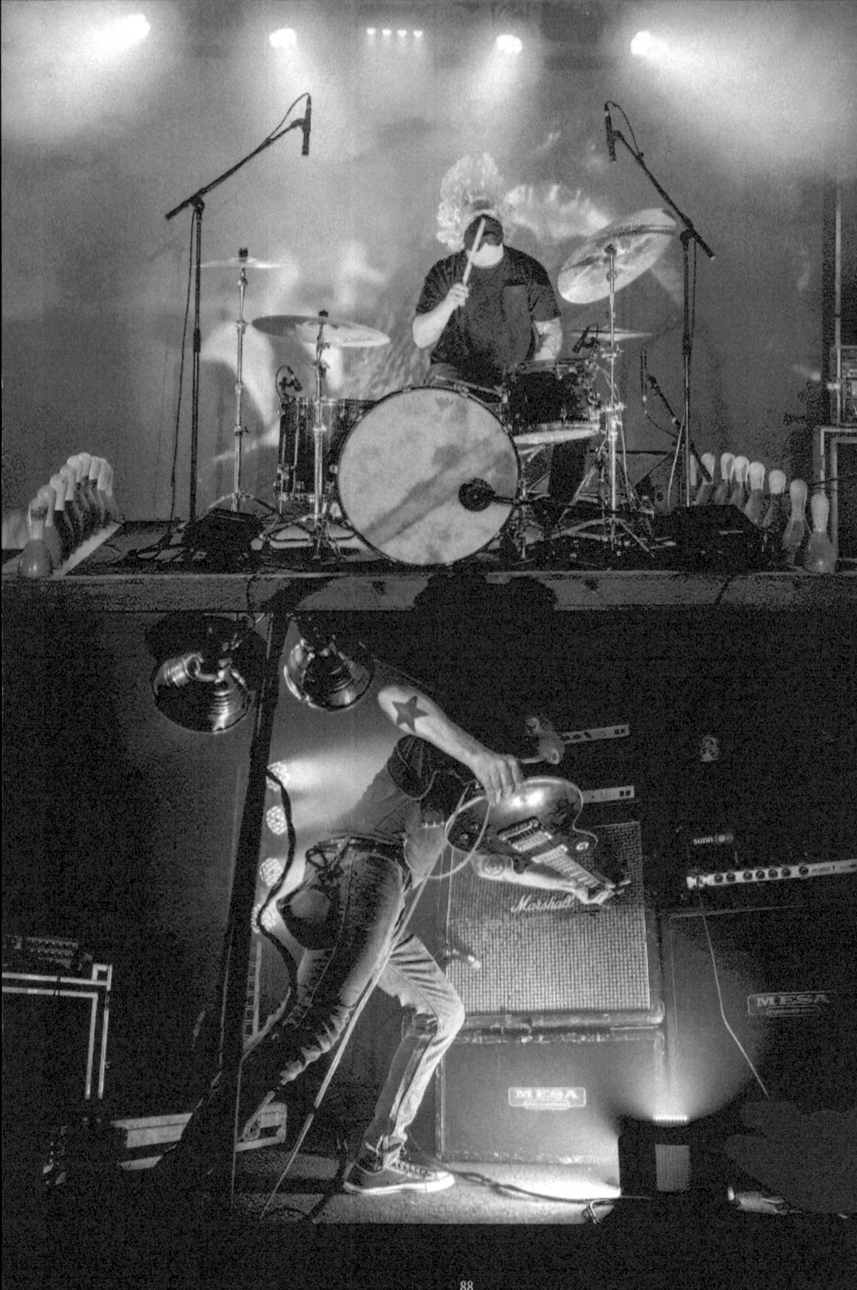
Marshall
MESA
MESA

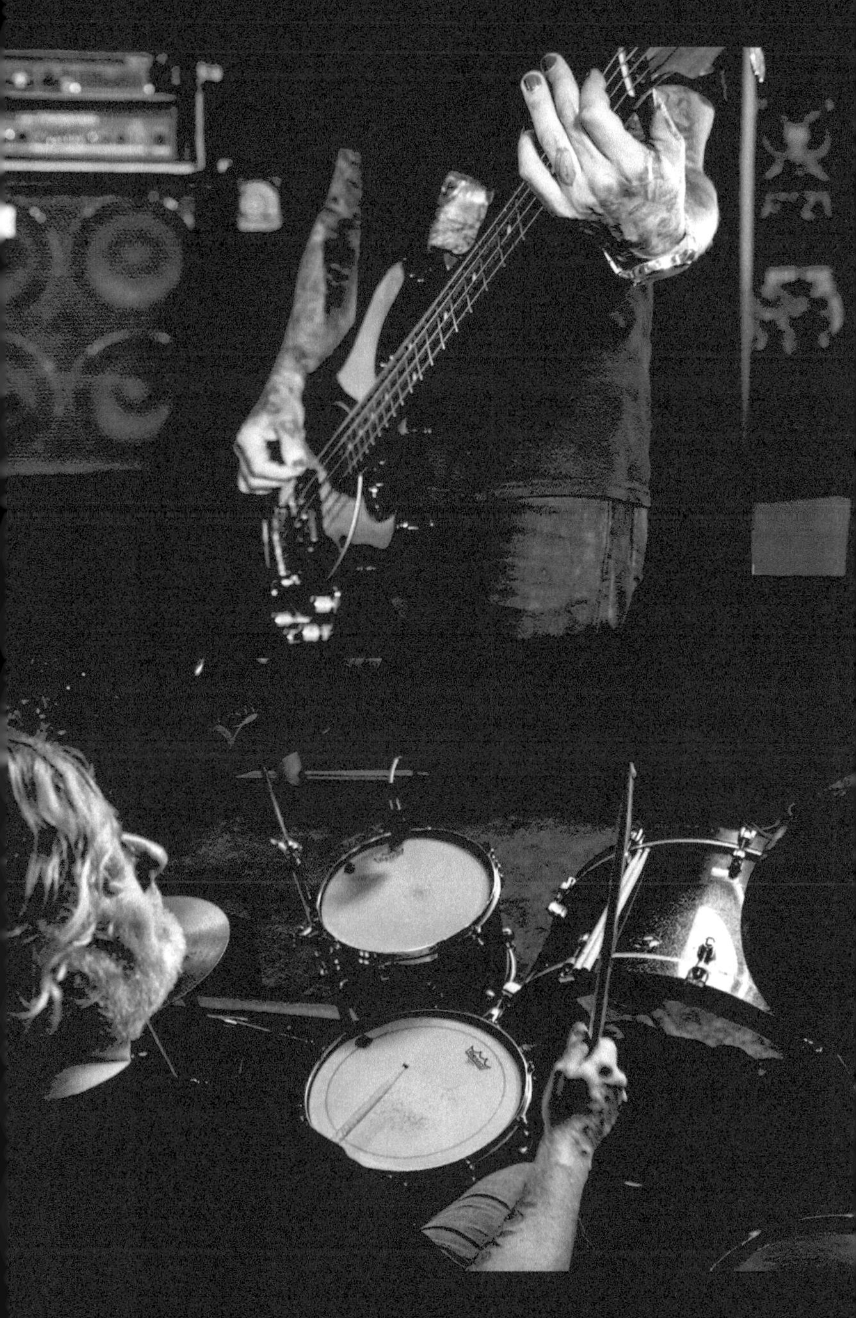

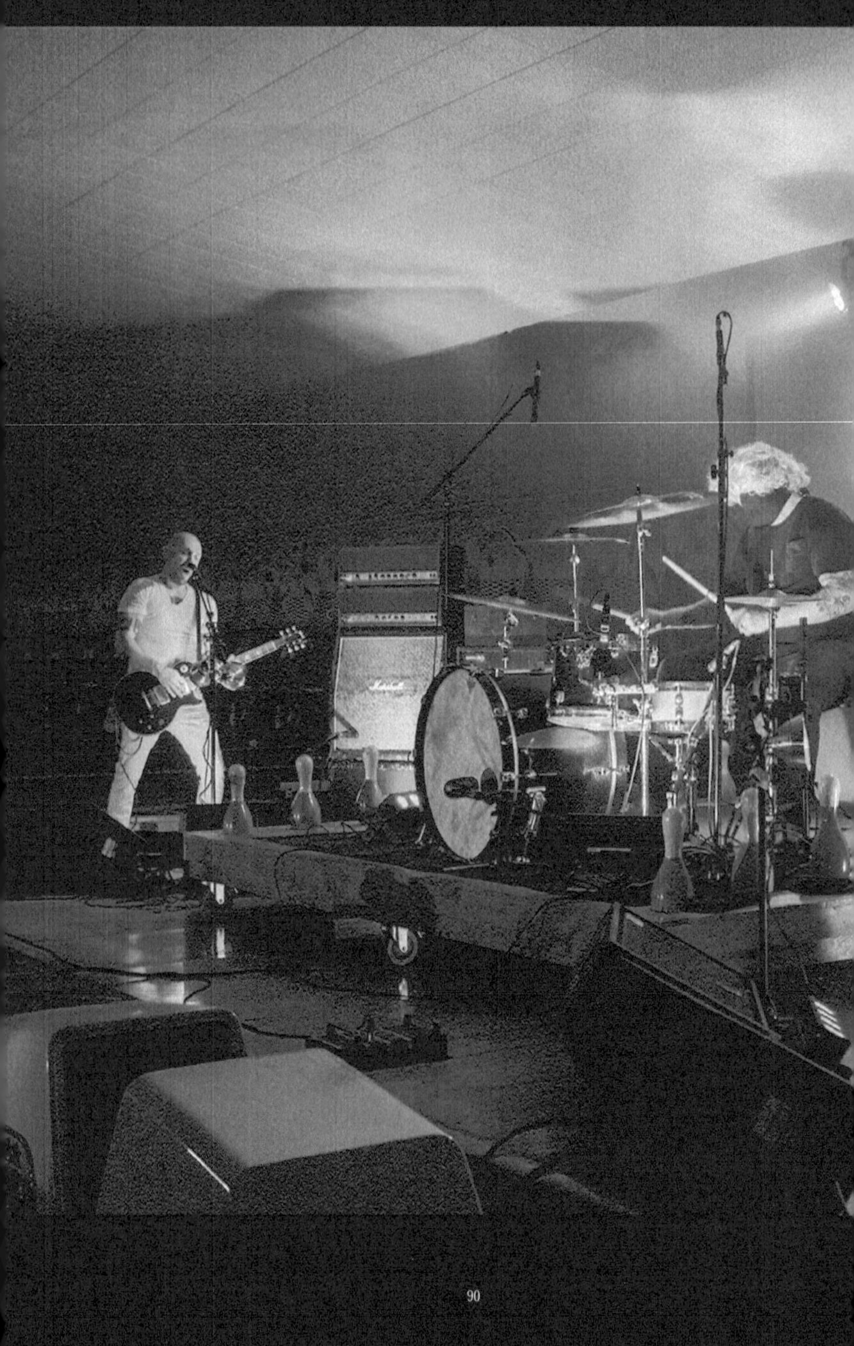

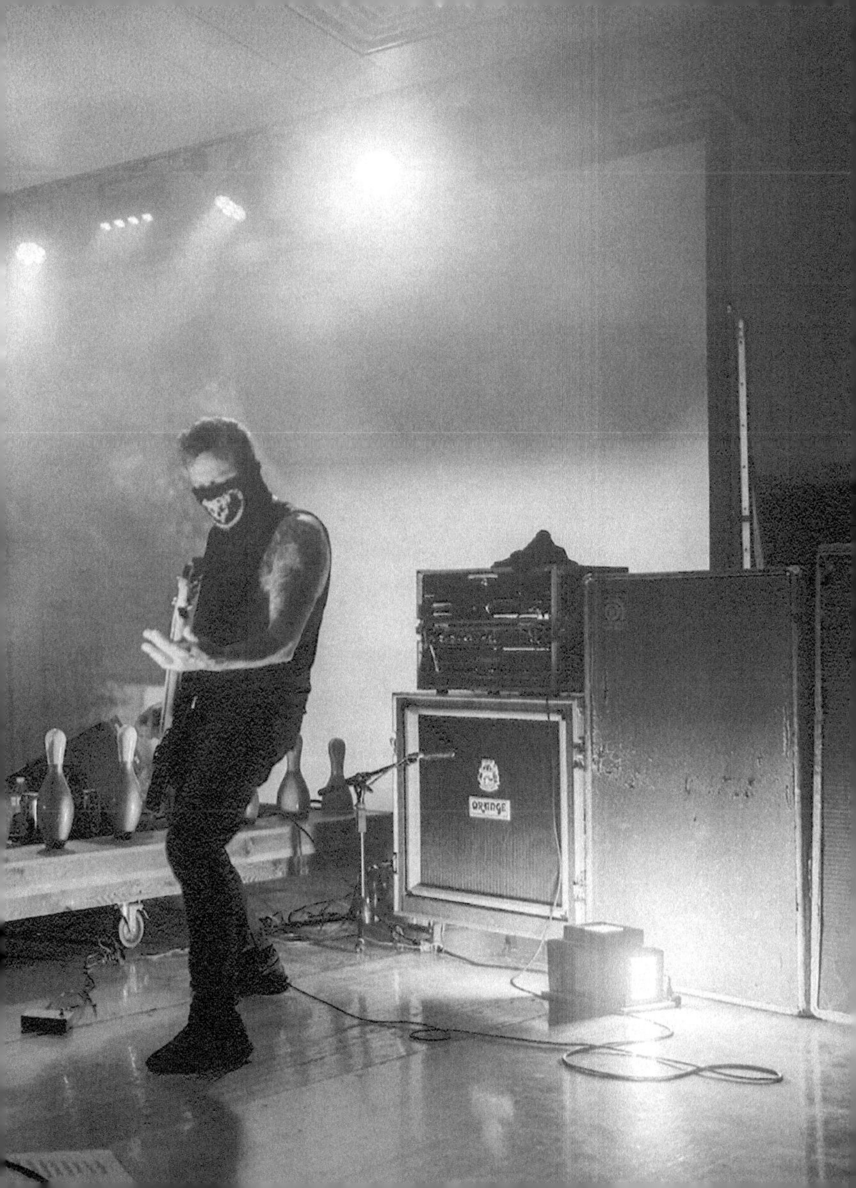
ORANGE

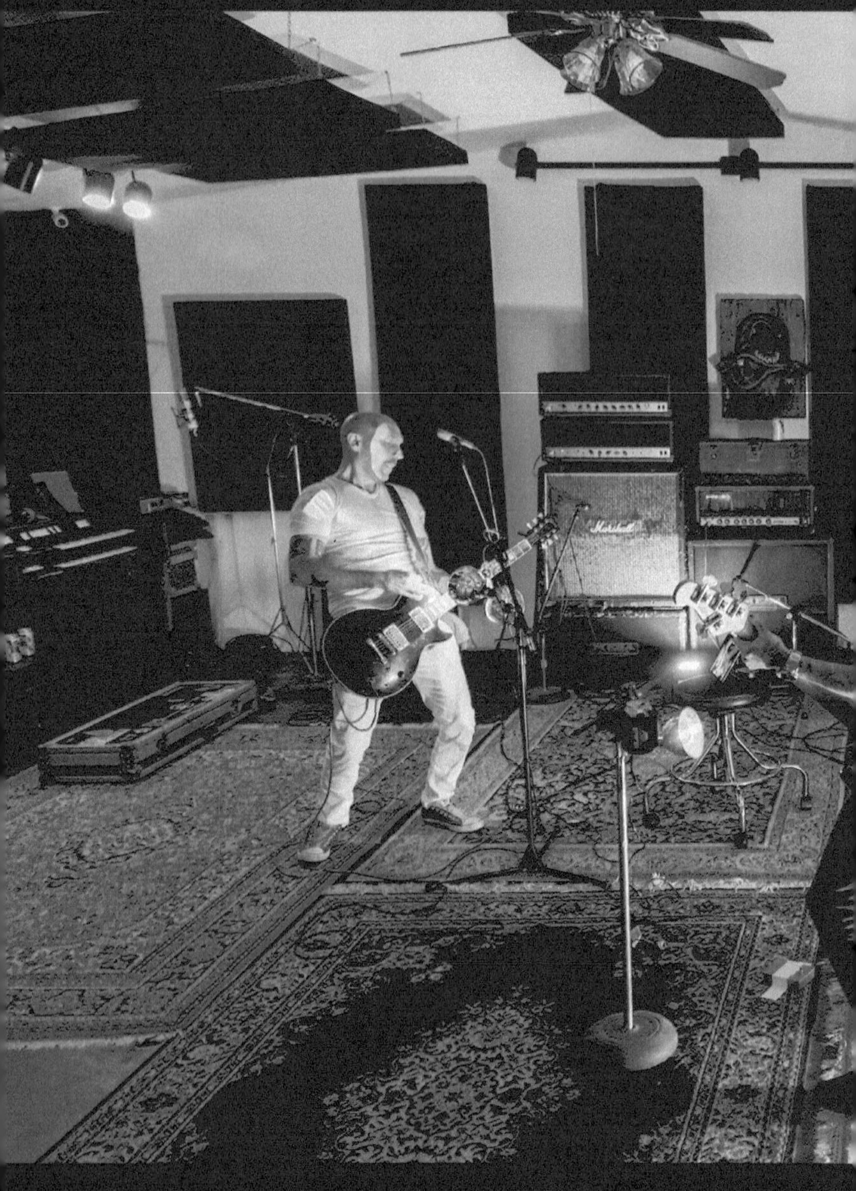
Marshall

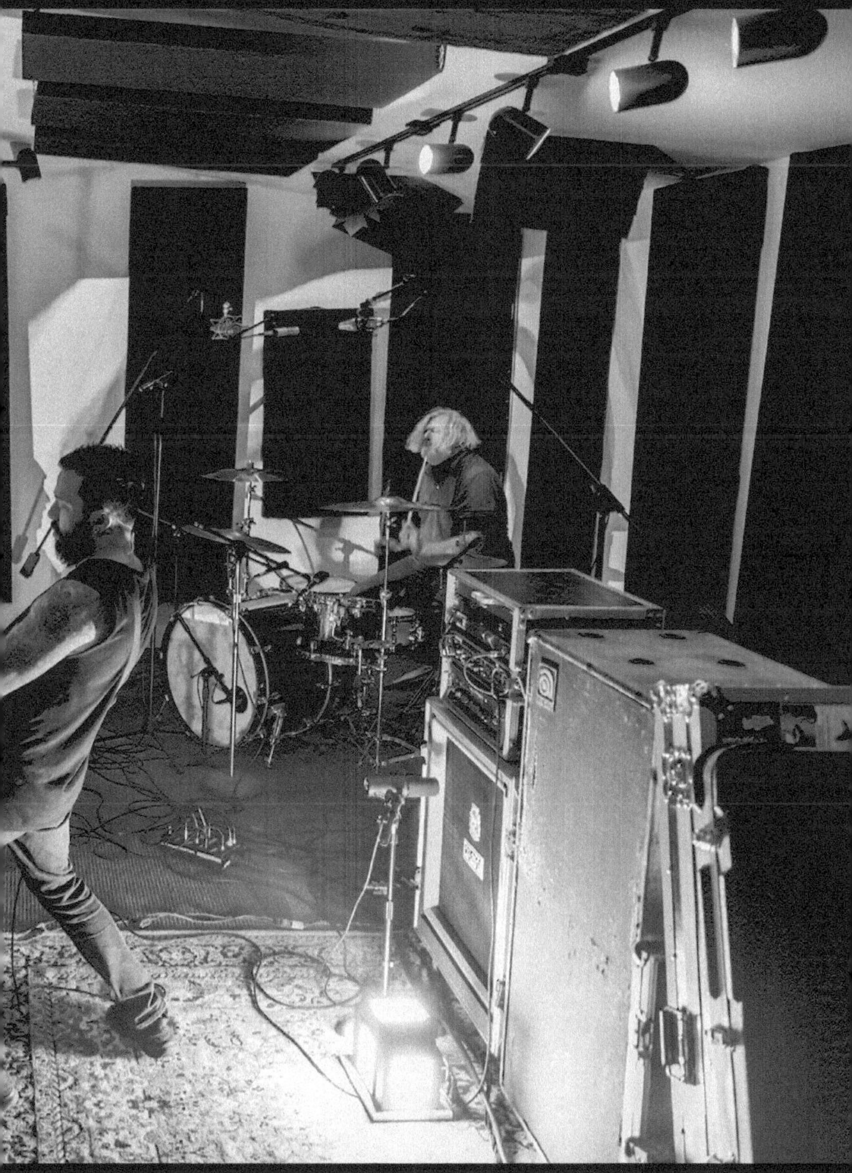

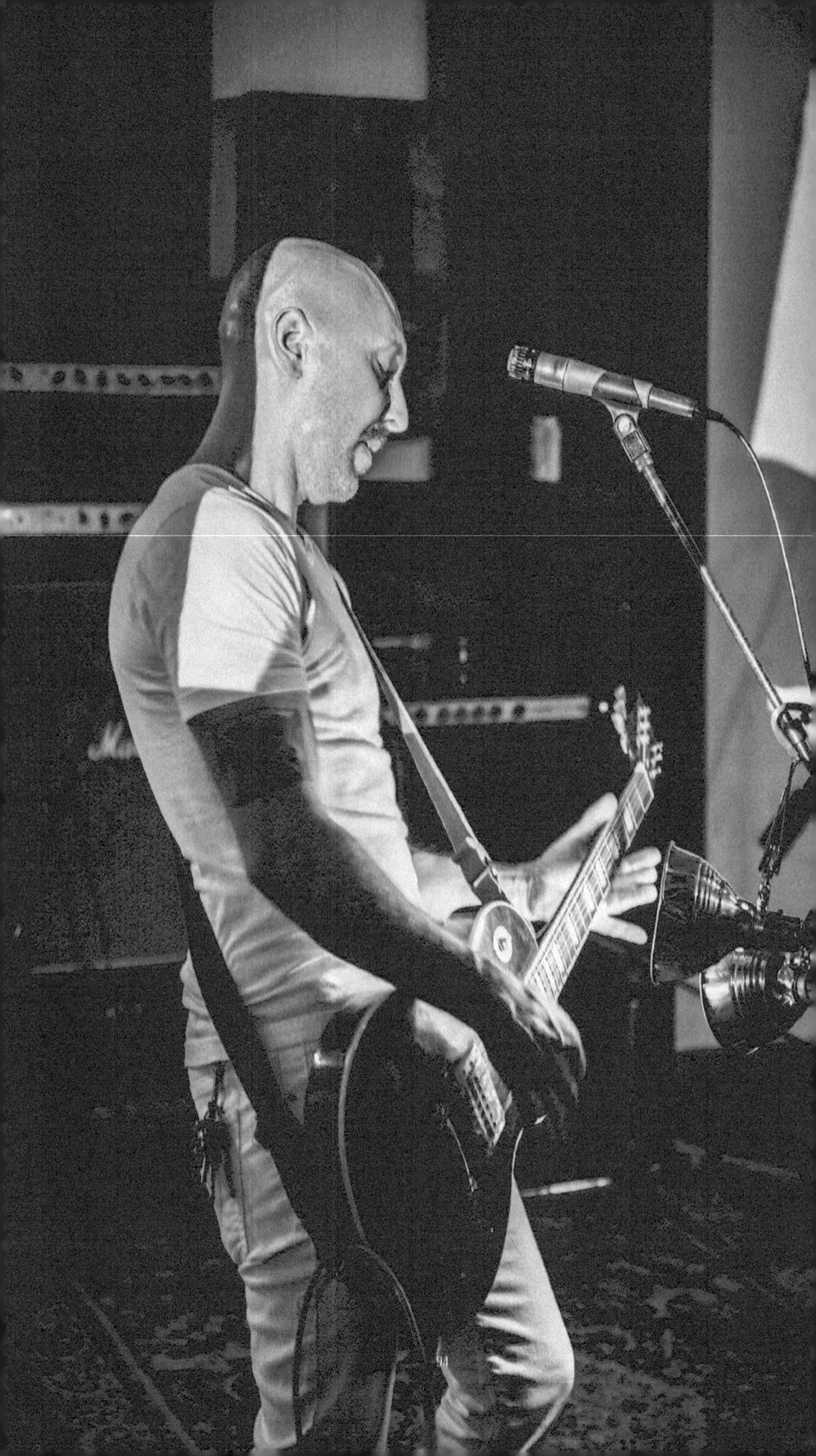

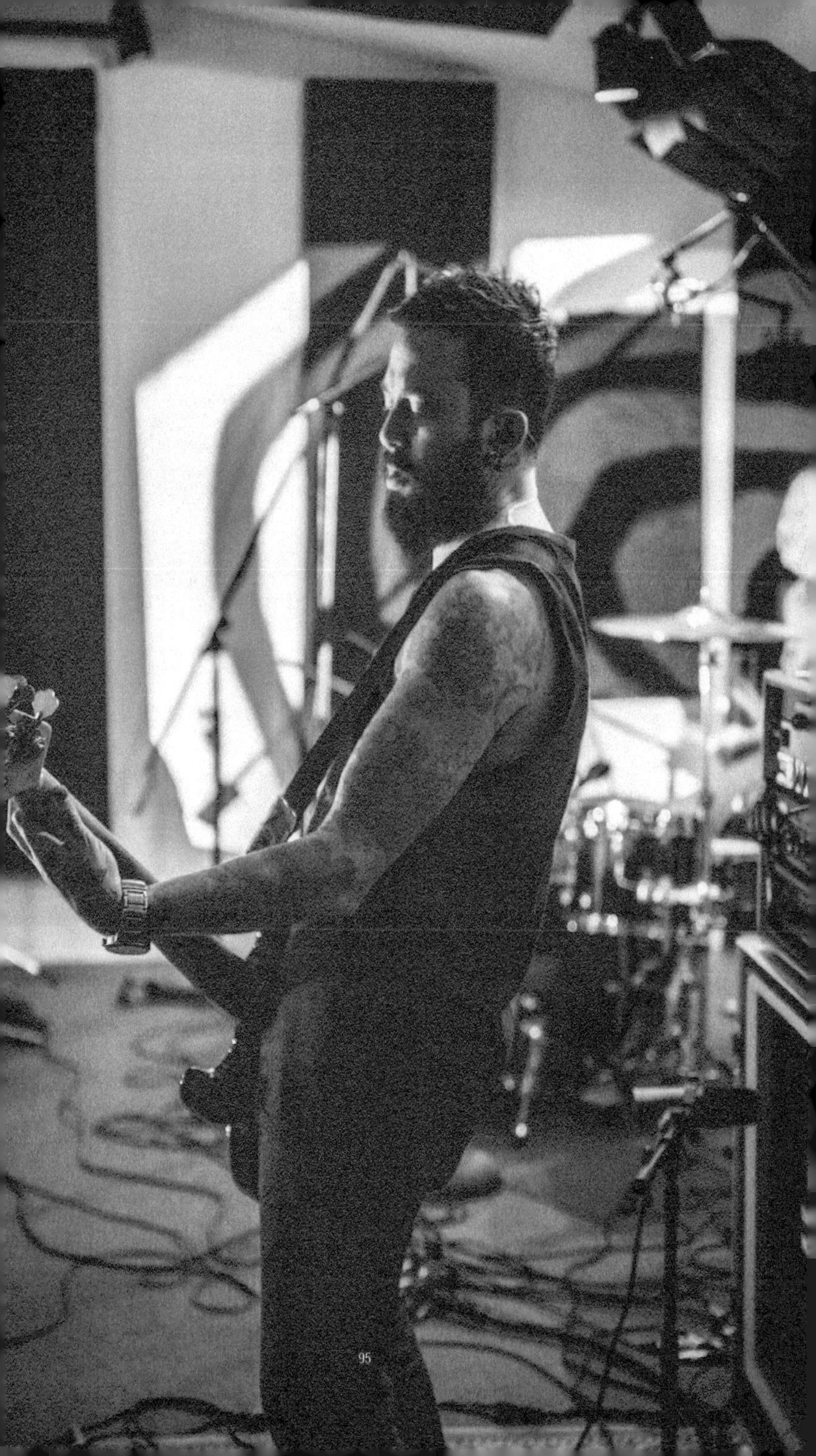

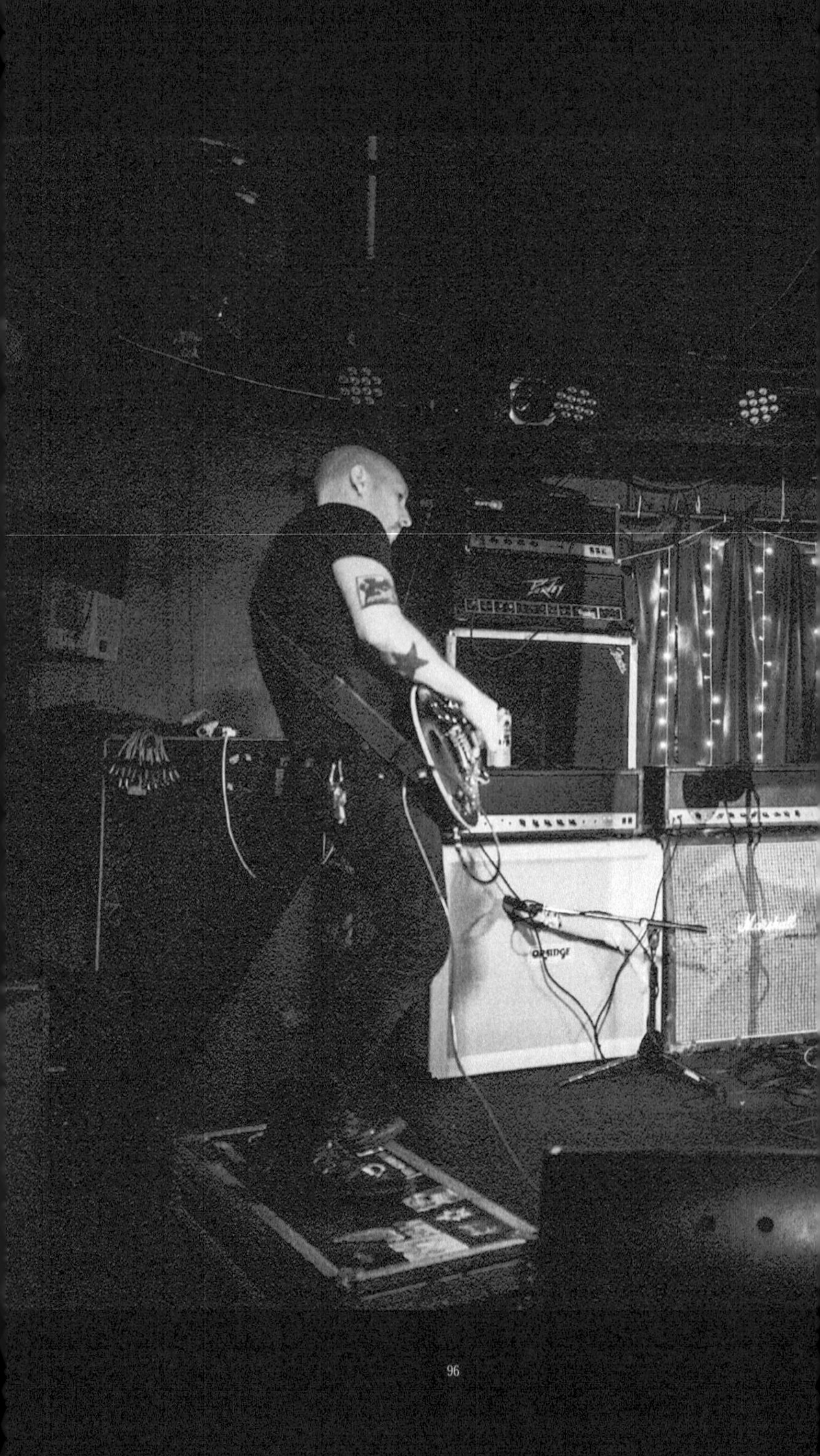
ORANGE

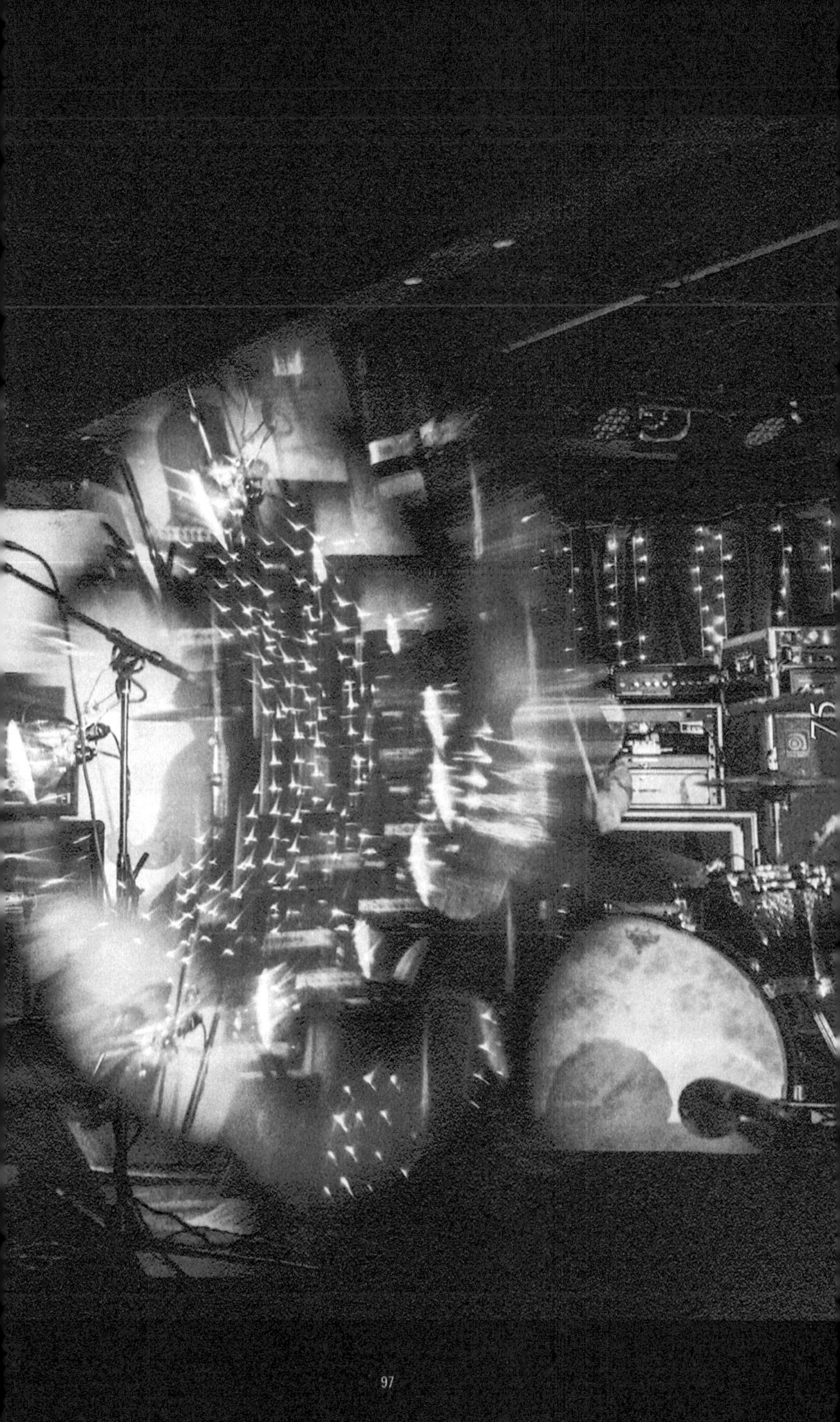

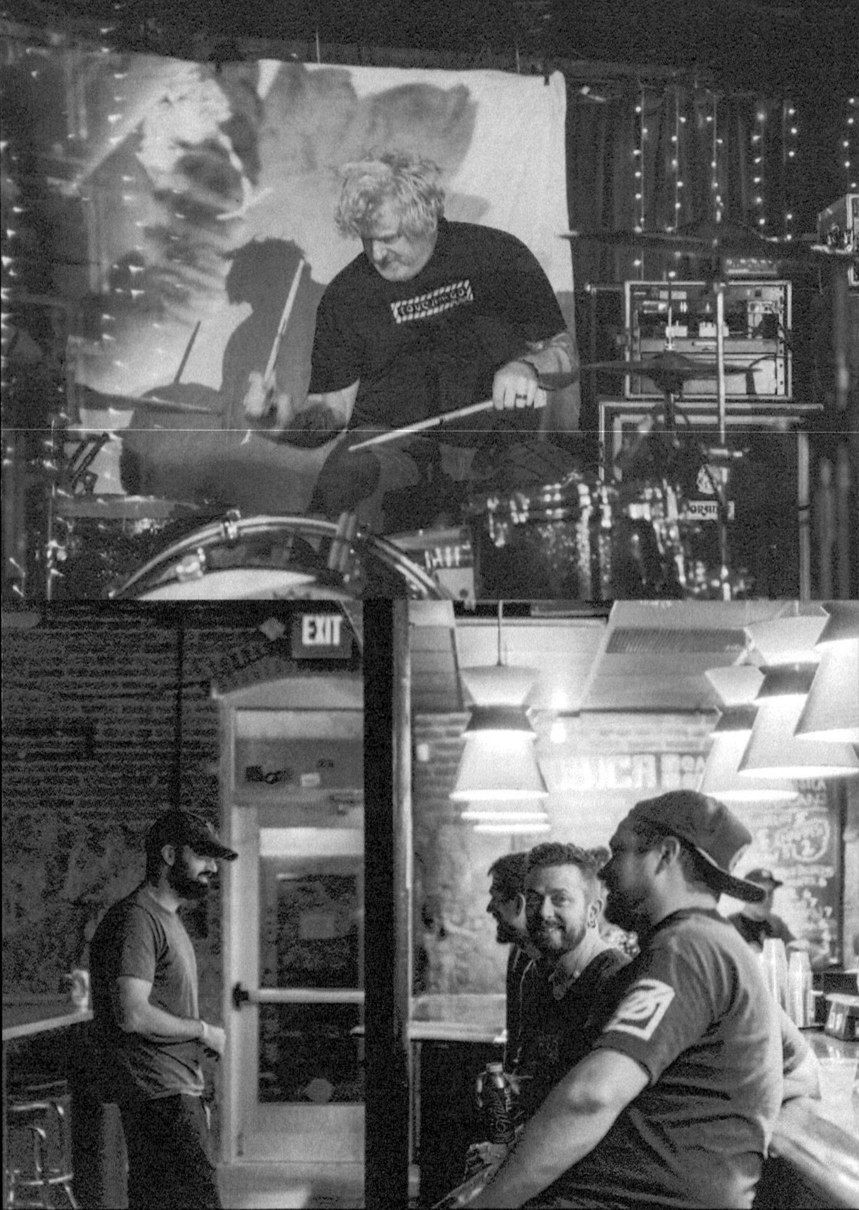
EXIT

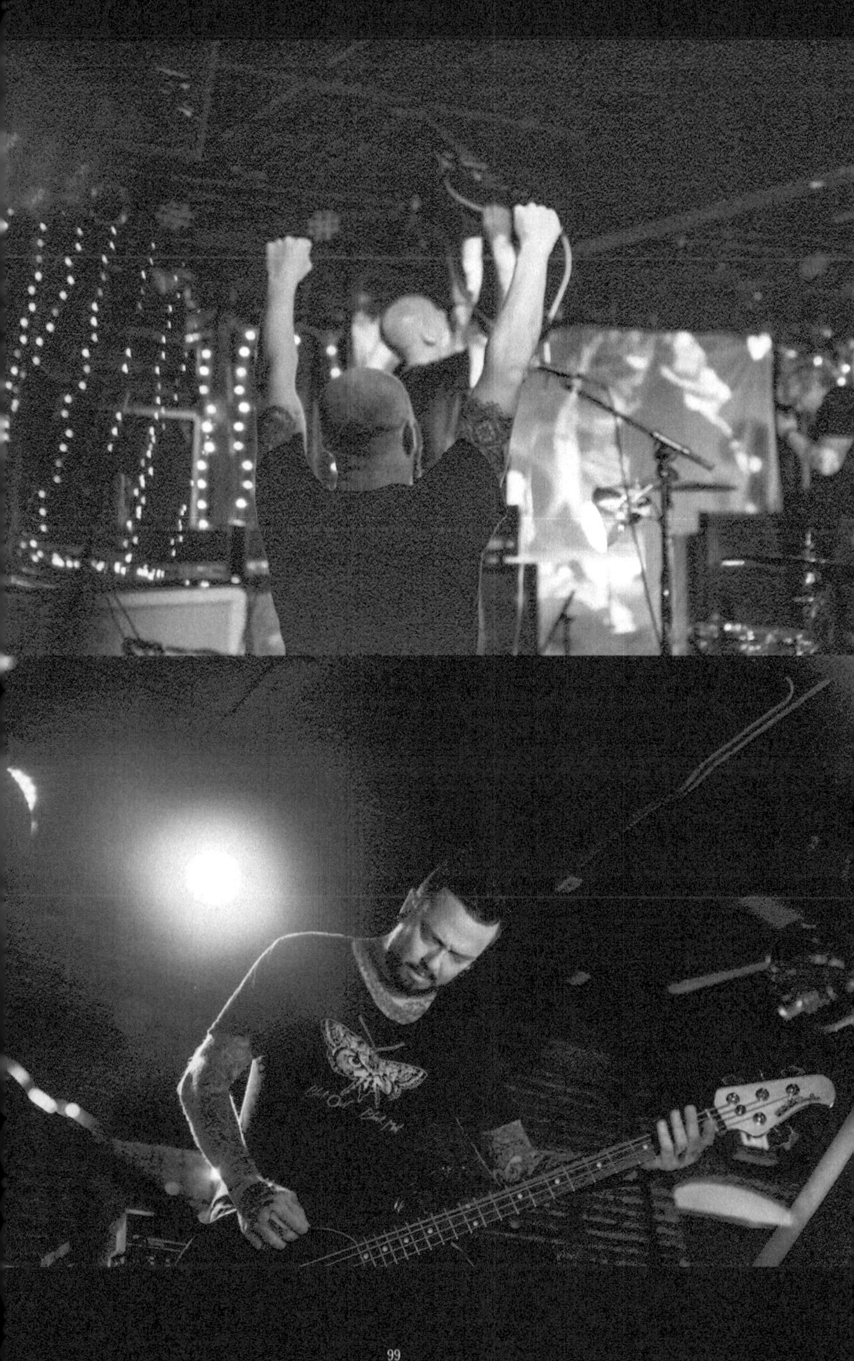

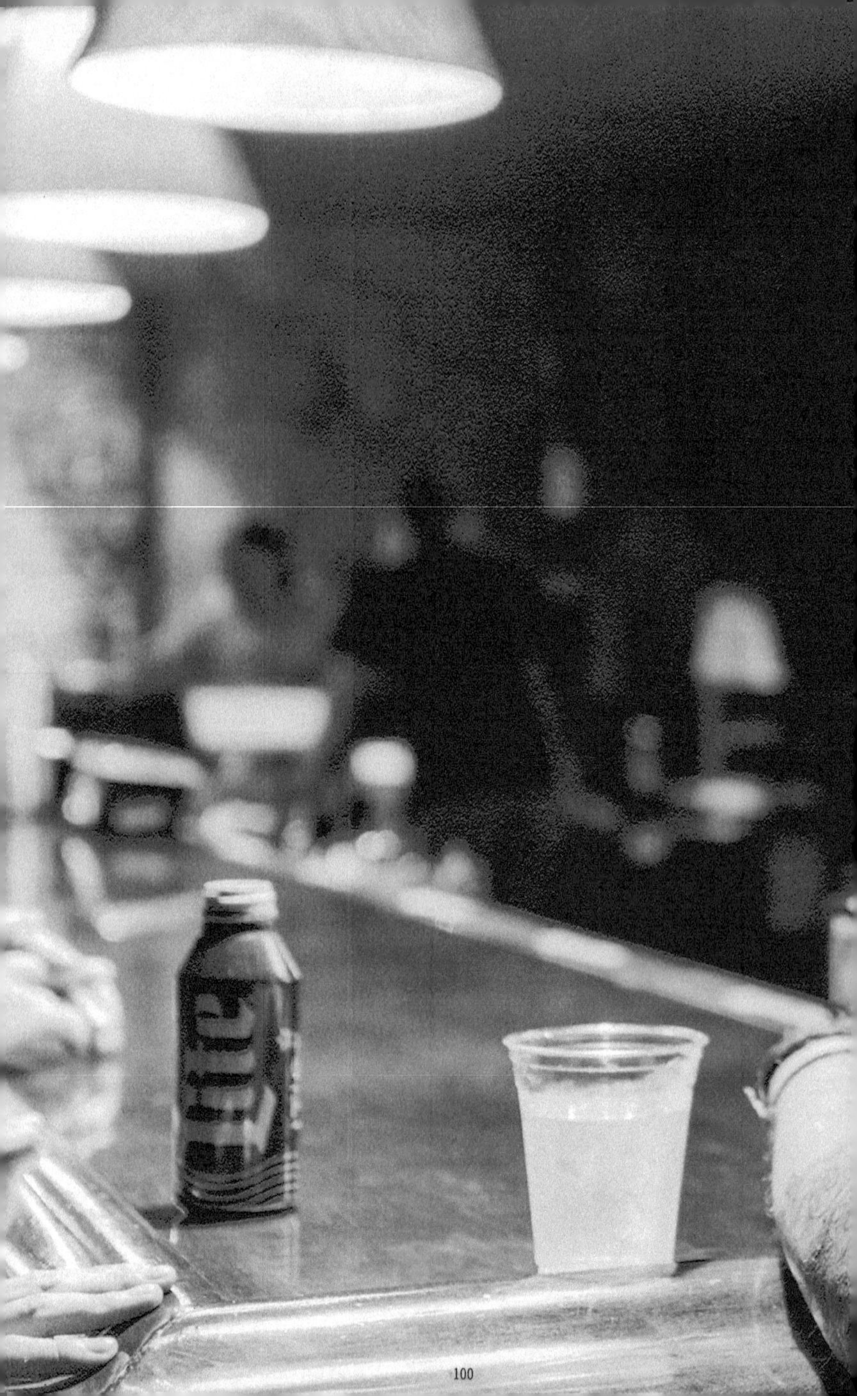
Lite

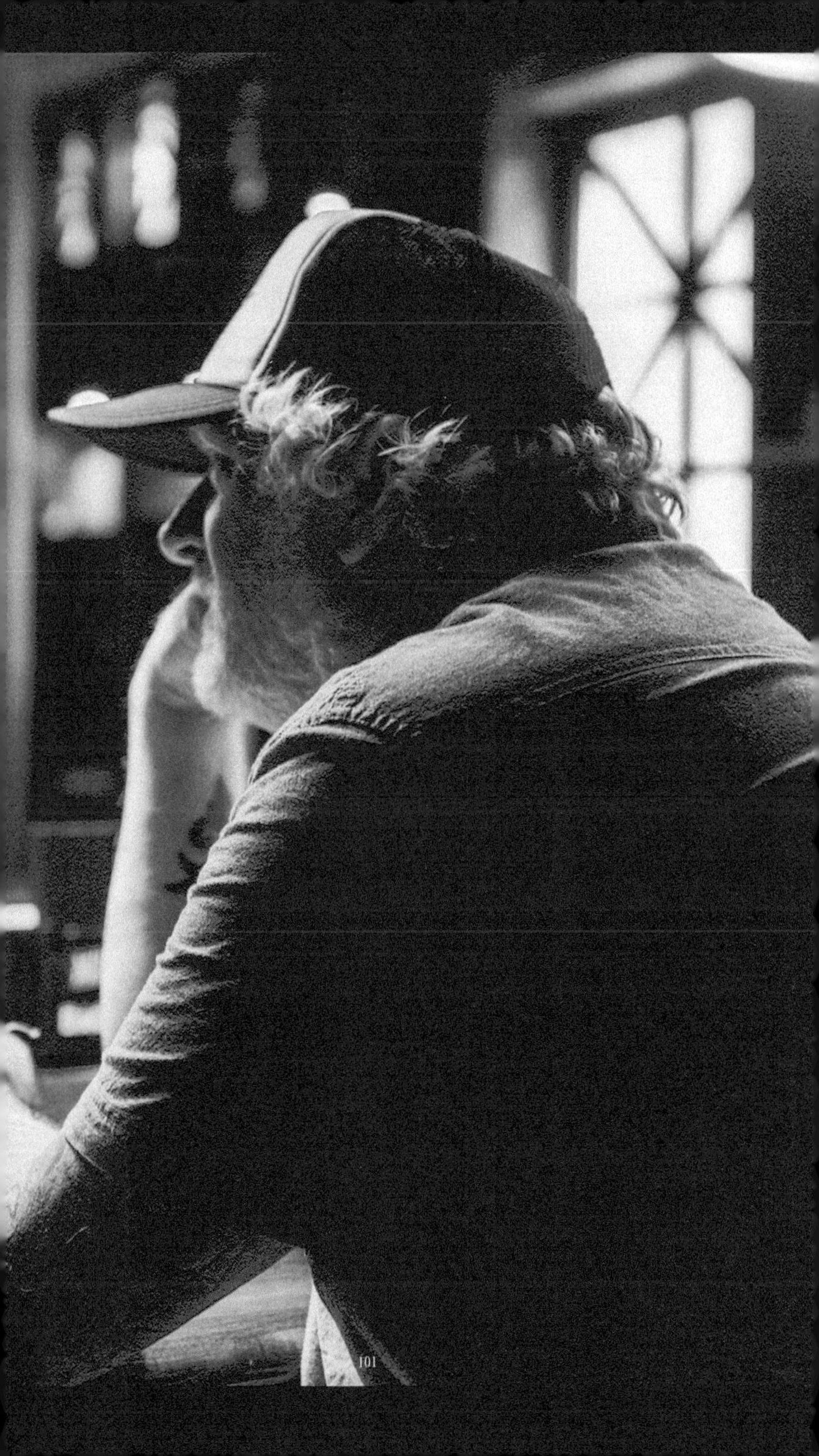

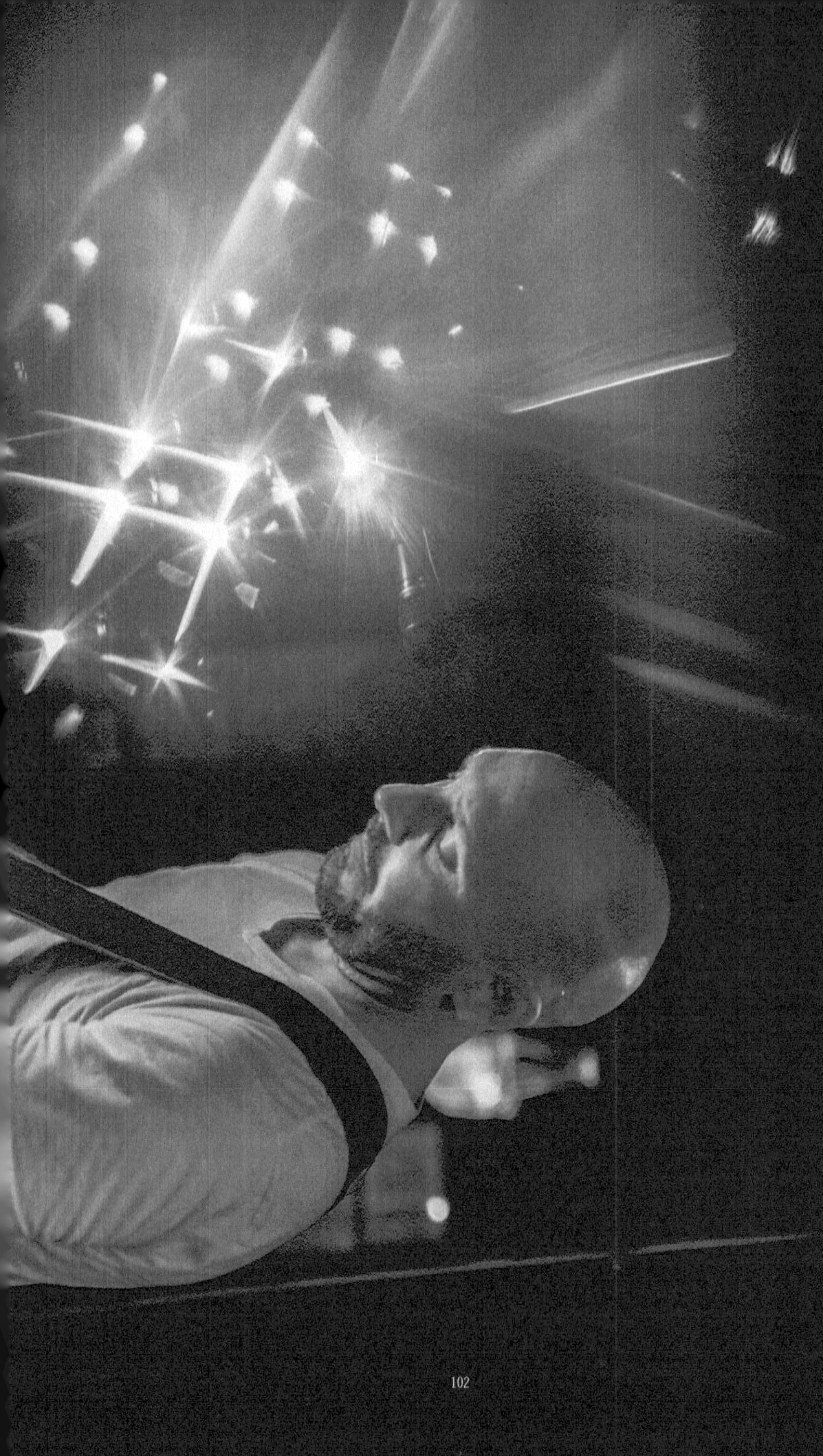

We spent an evening with Mollie at Westside Bowl during the shutdown of Fall 2020.

These are some of the results of that magical night...

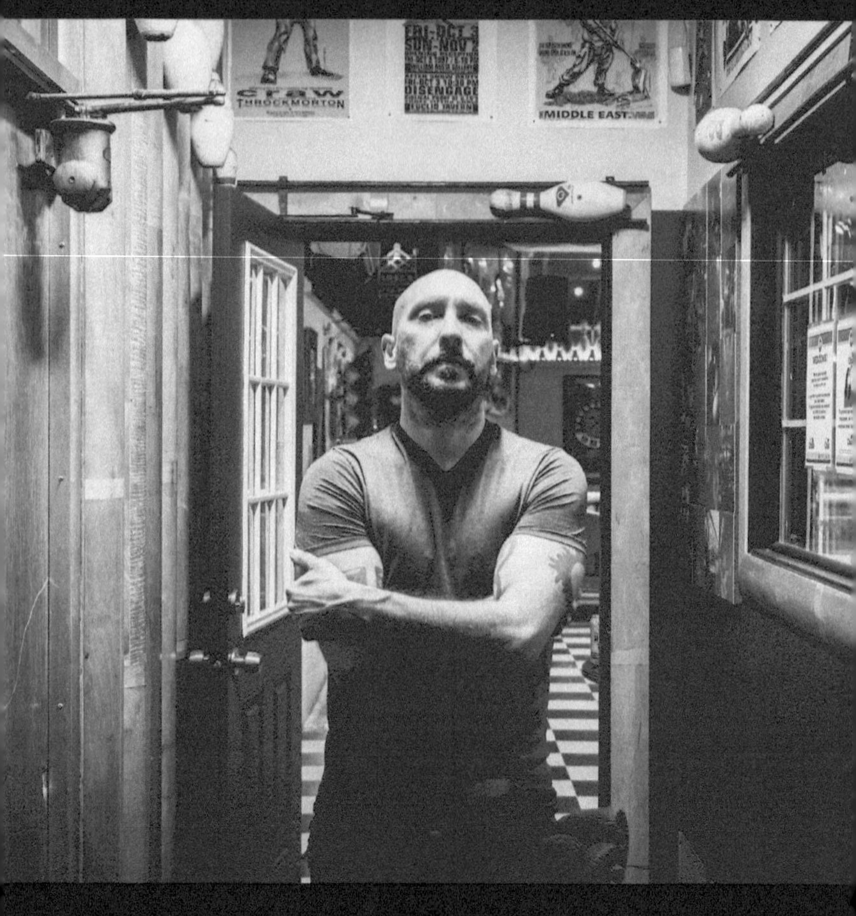
craw
THROCKMORTON
FRI-OCT 3
SUN-NOV 2
DISENGAGE
MIDDLE EAST.

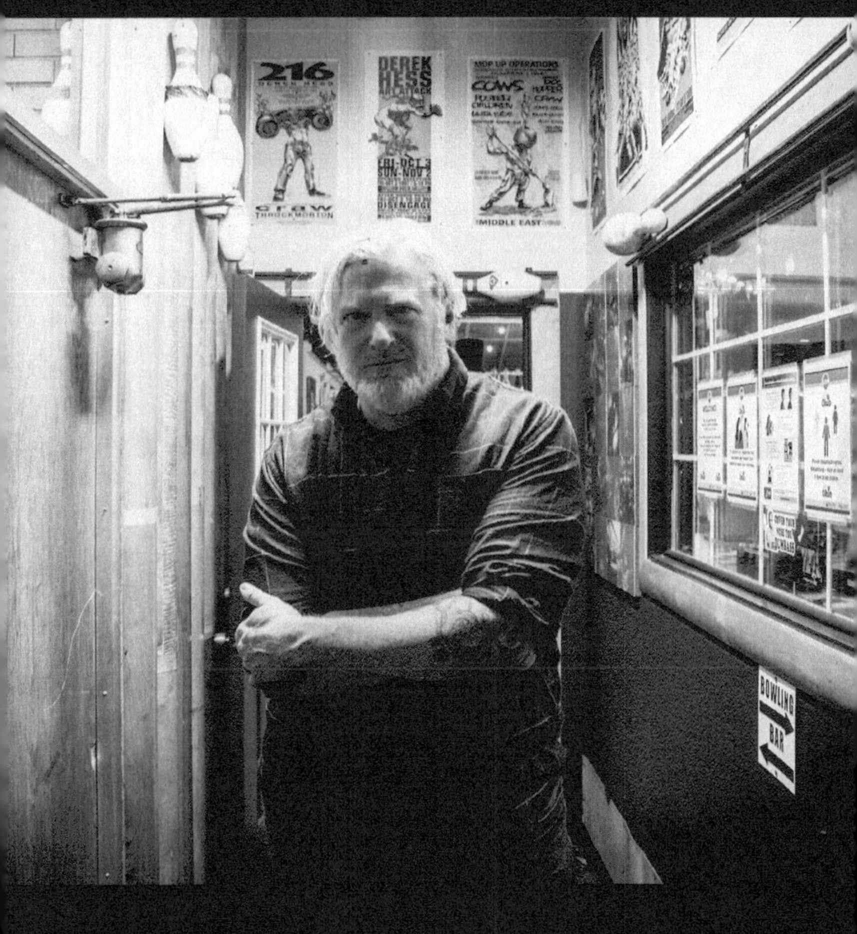
216
DEREK HESS
THROCKMORTON
FRI-OCT 3
SUN-NOV 2
MOP UP OPERATIONS
COWS
MIDDLE EAST
BOWLING
BAR

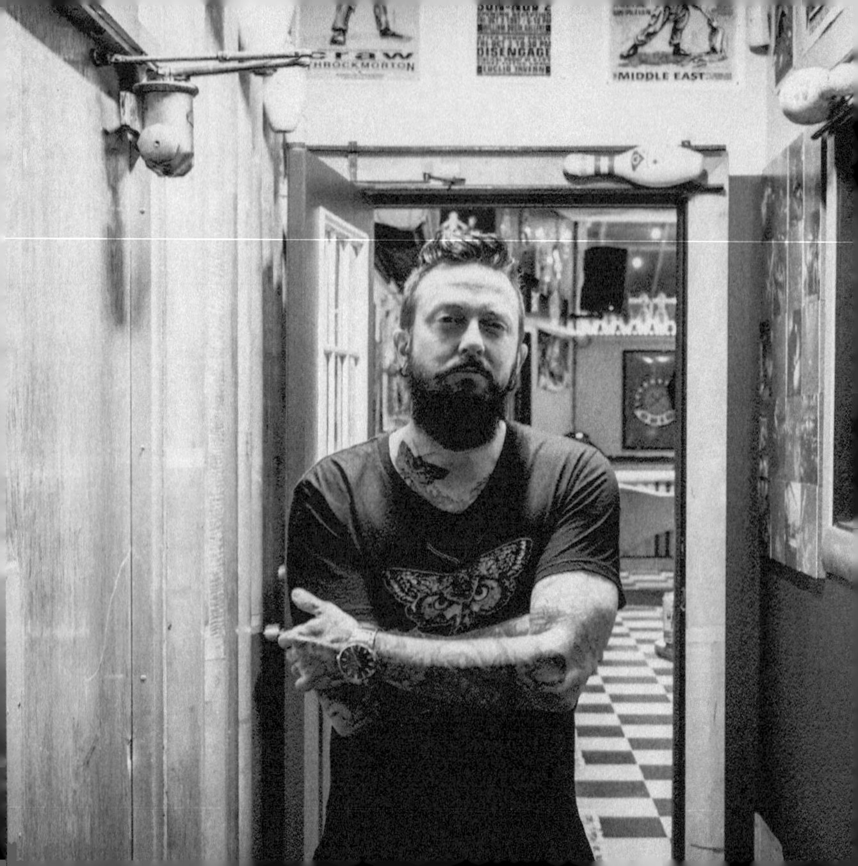
craw
DISENGAGE
MIDDLE EAST

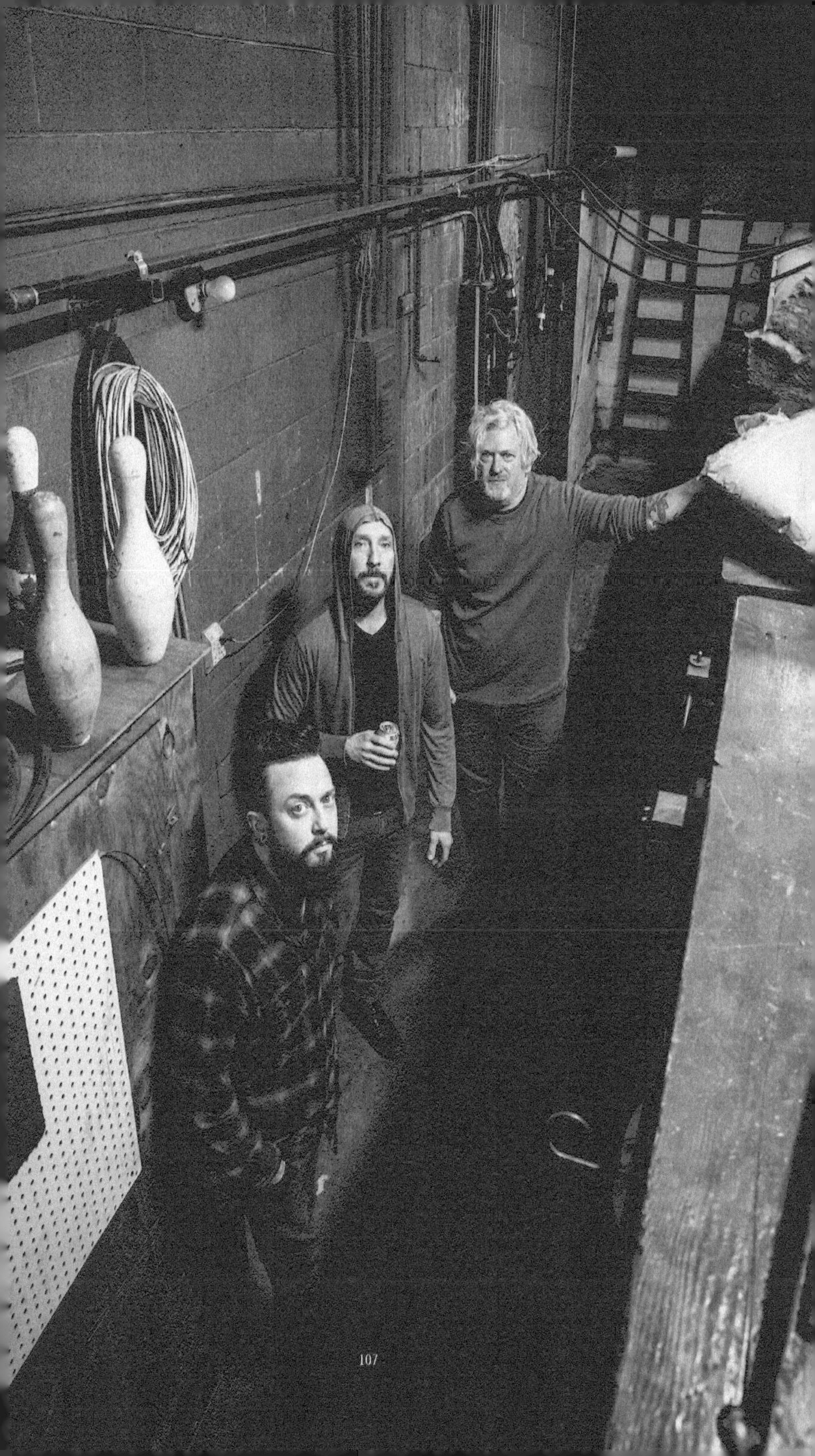

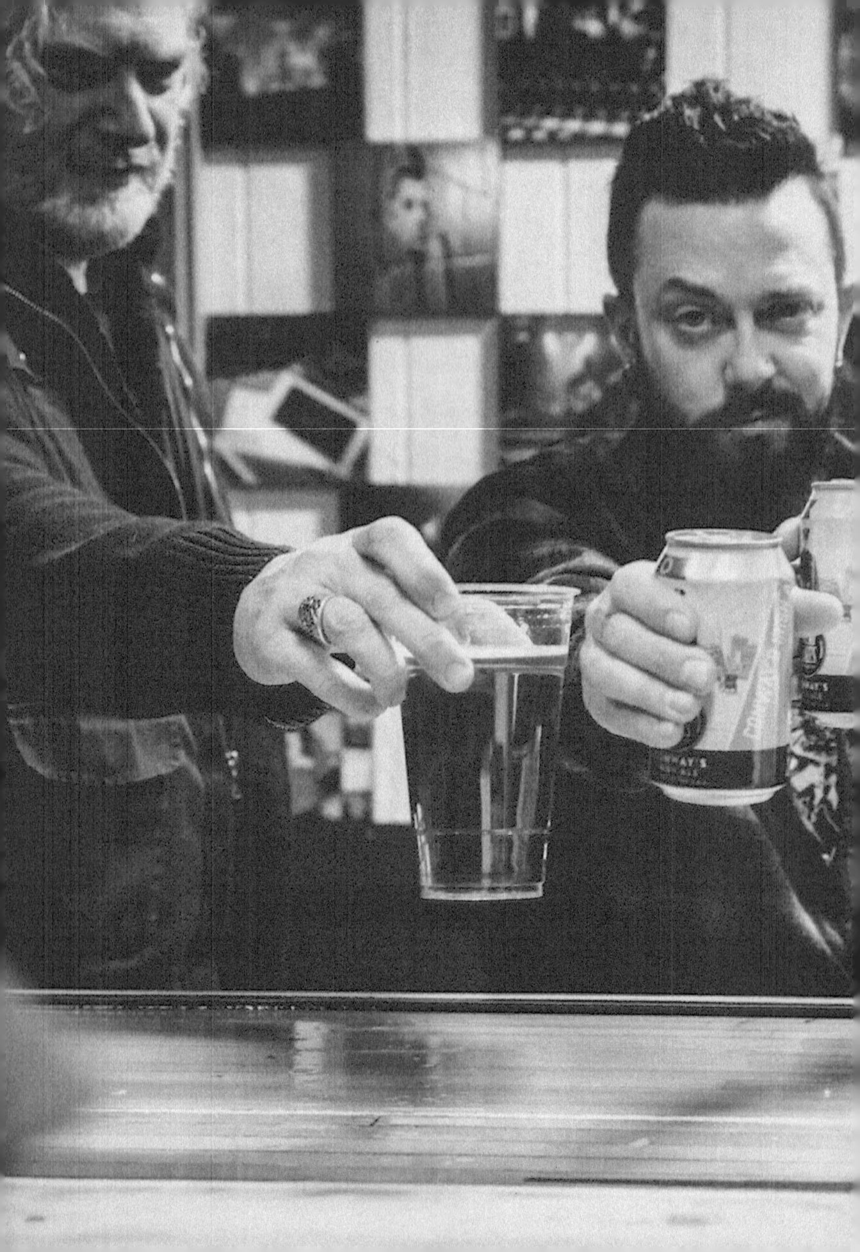

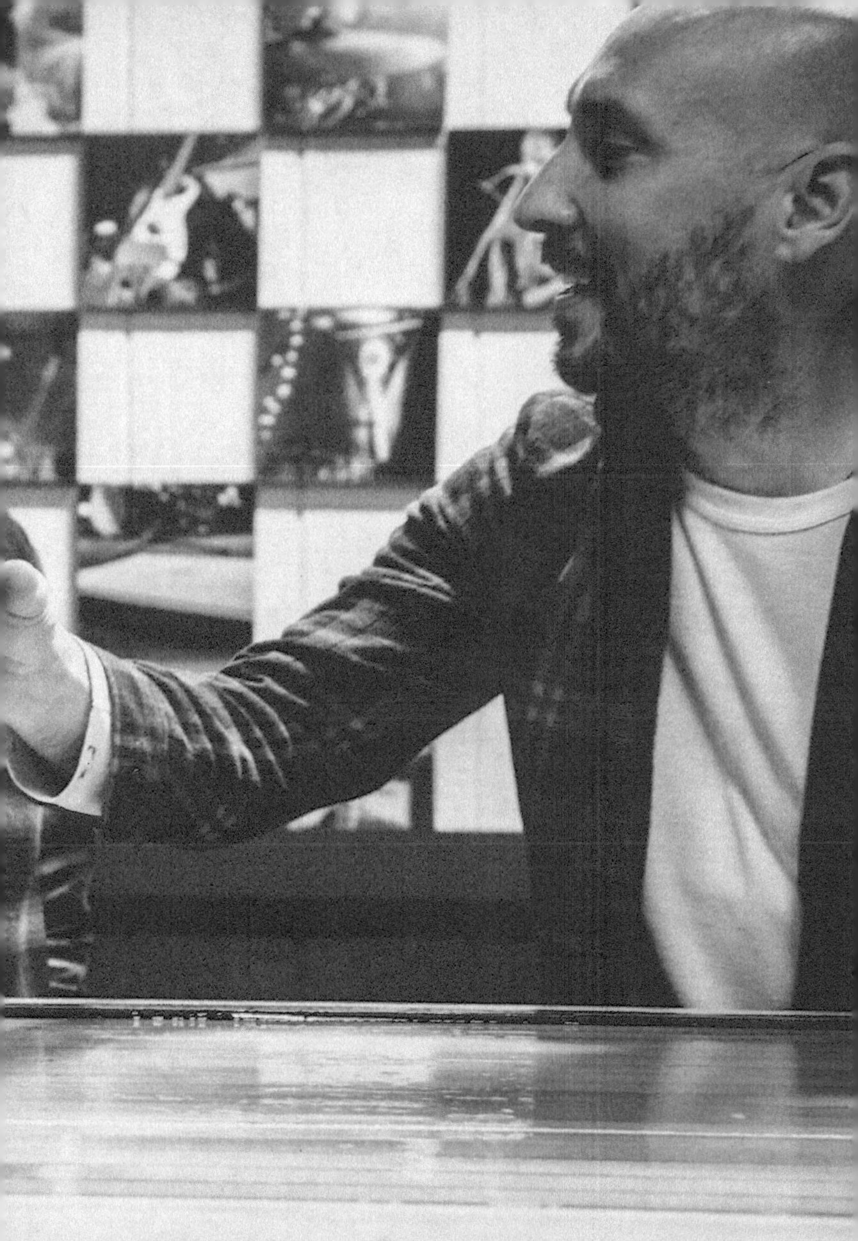

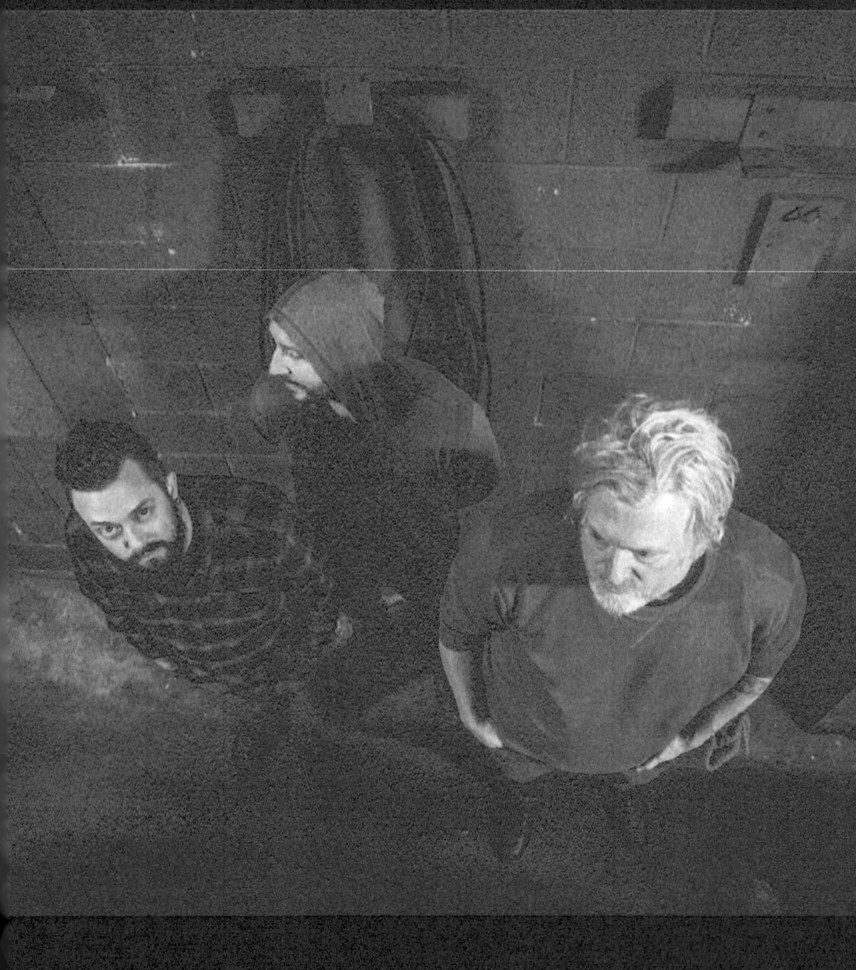

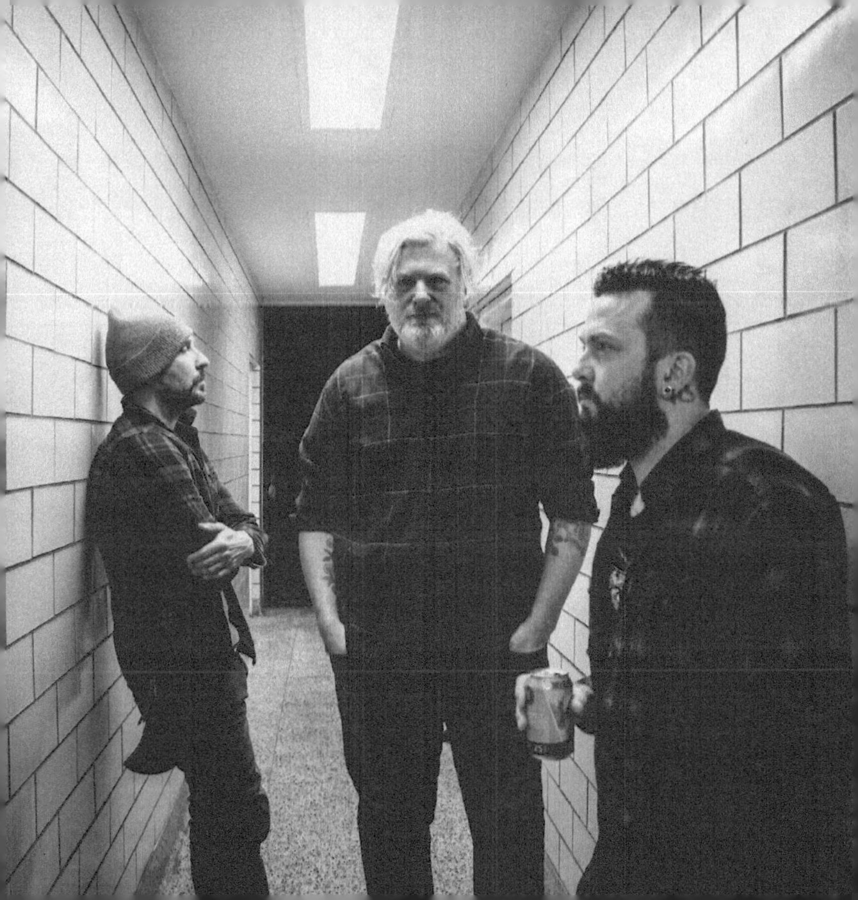

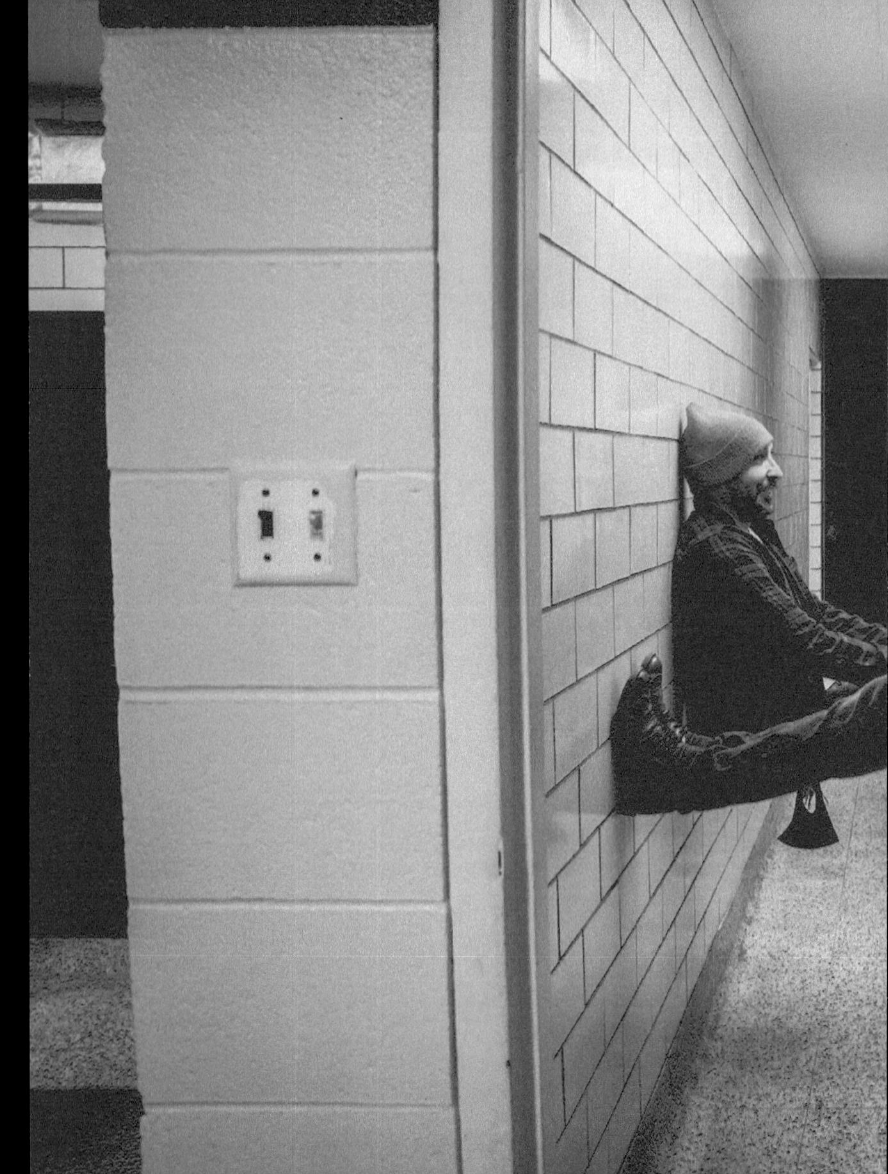

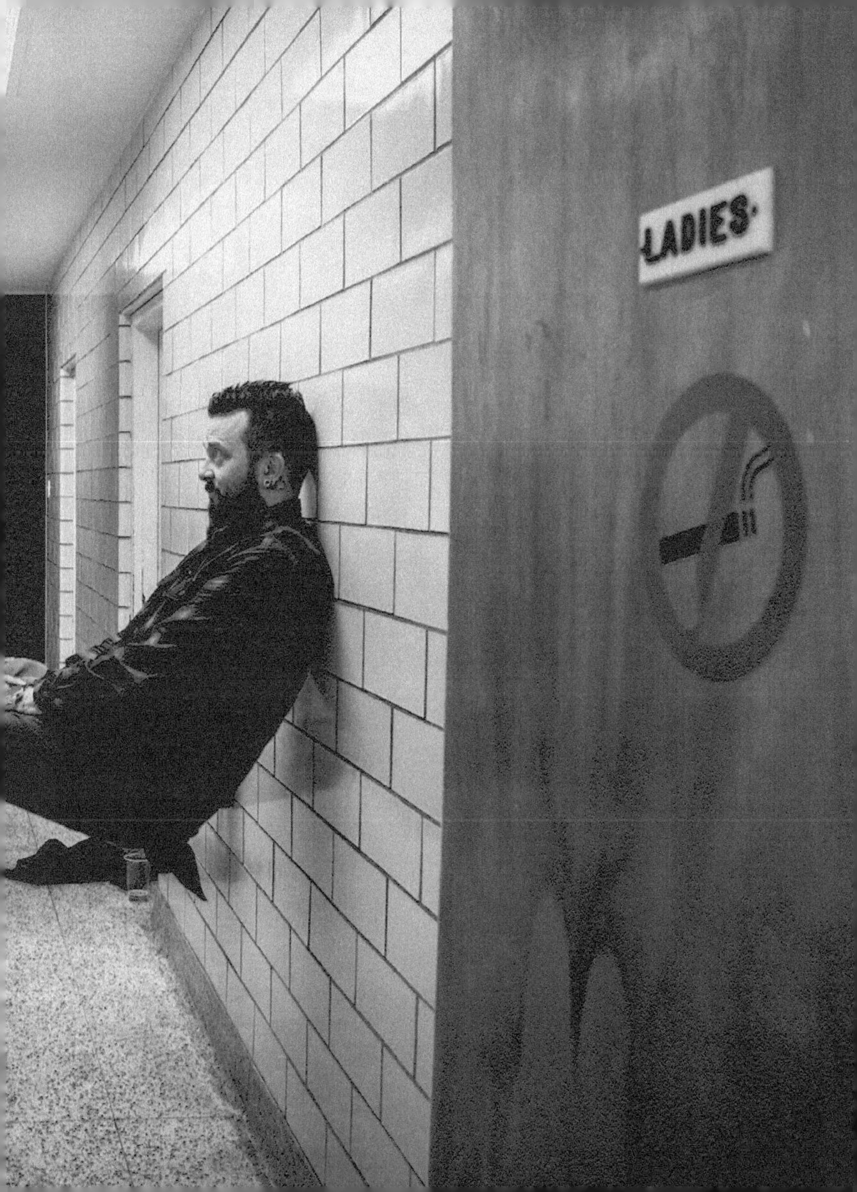
LADIES.

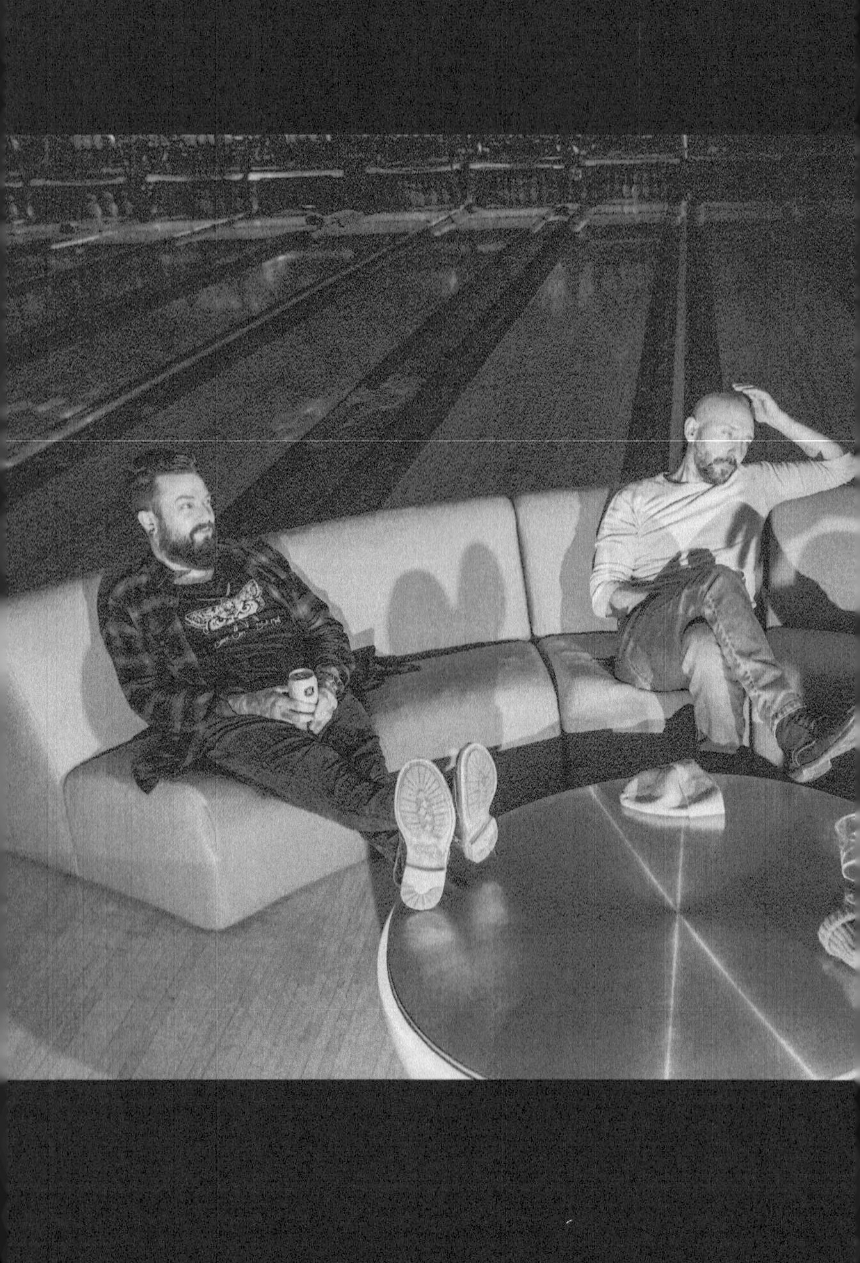

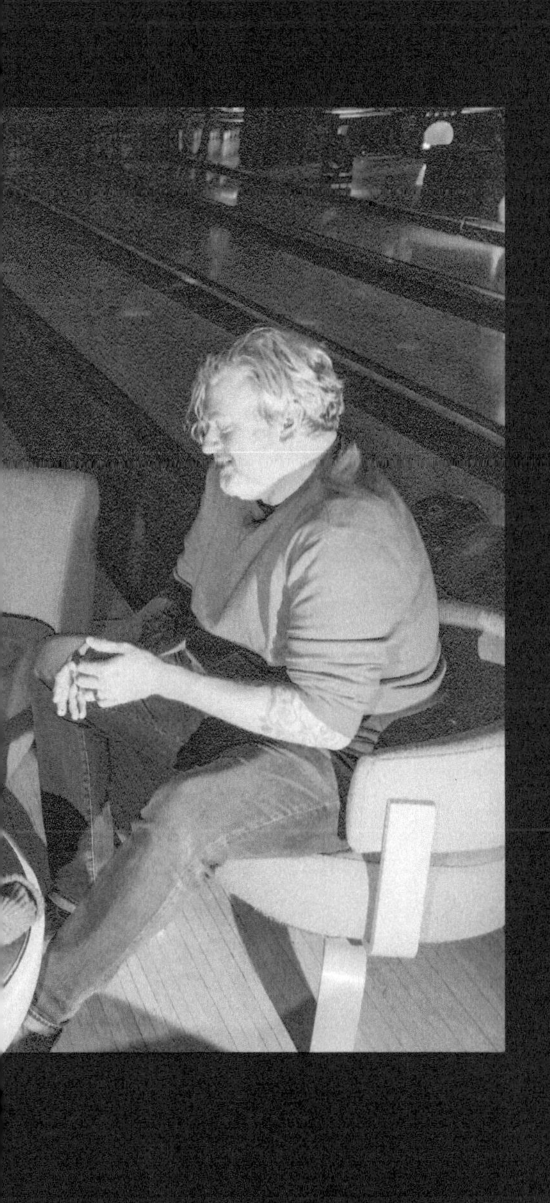

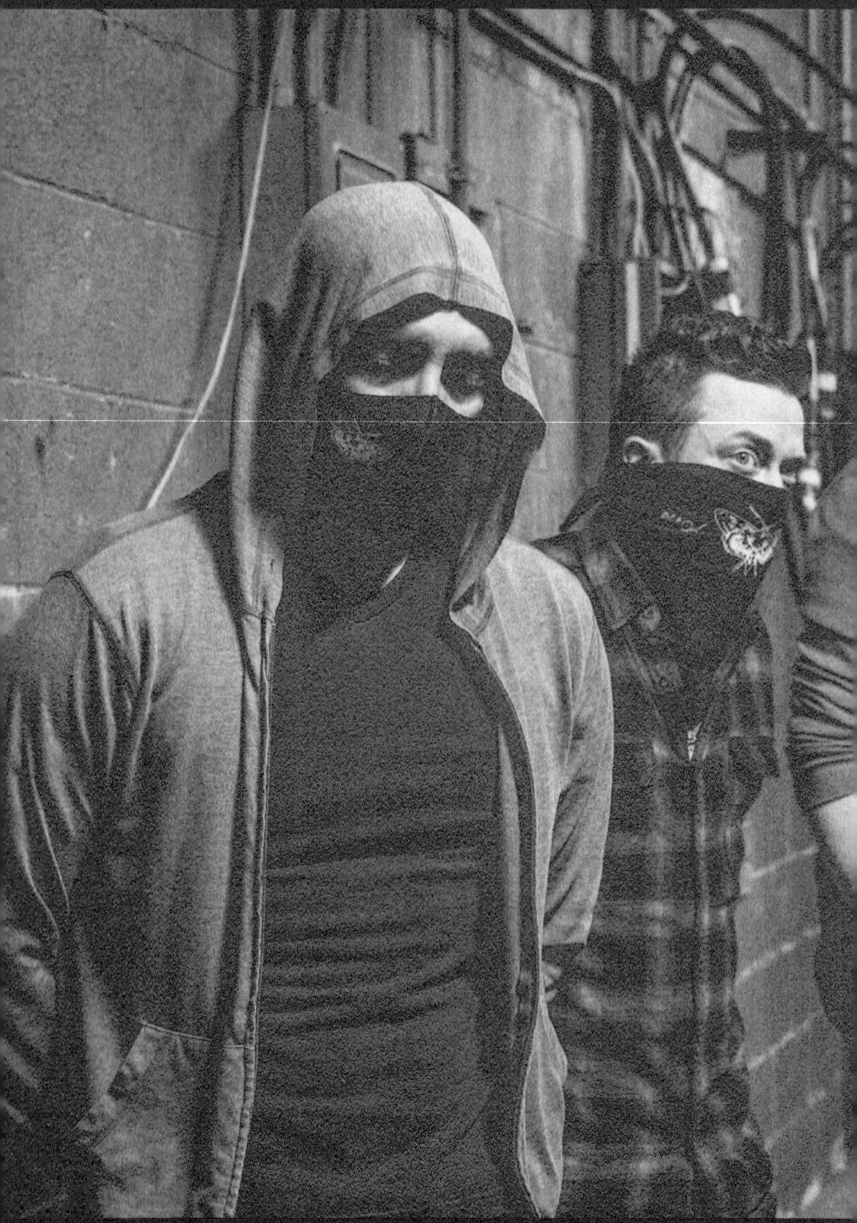

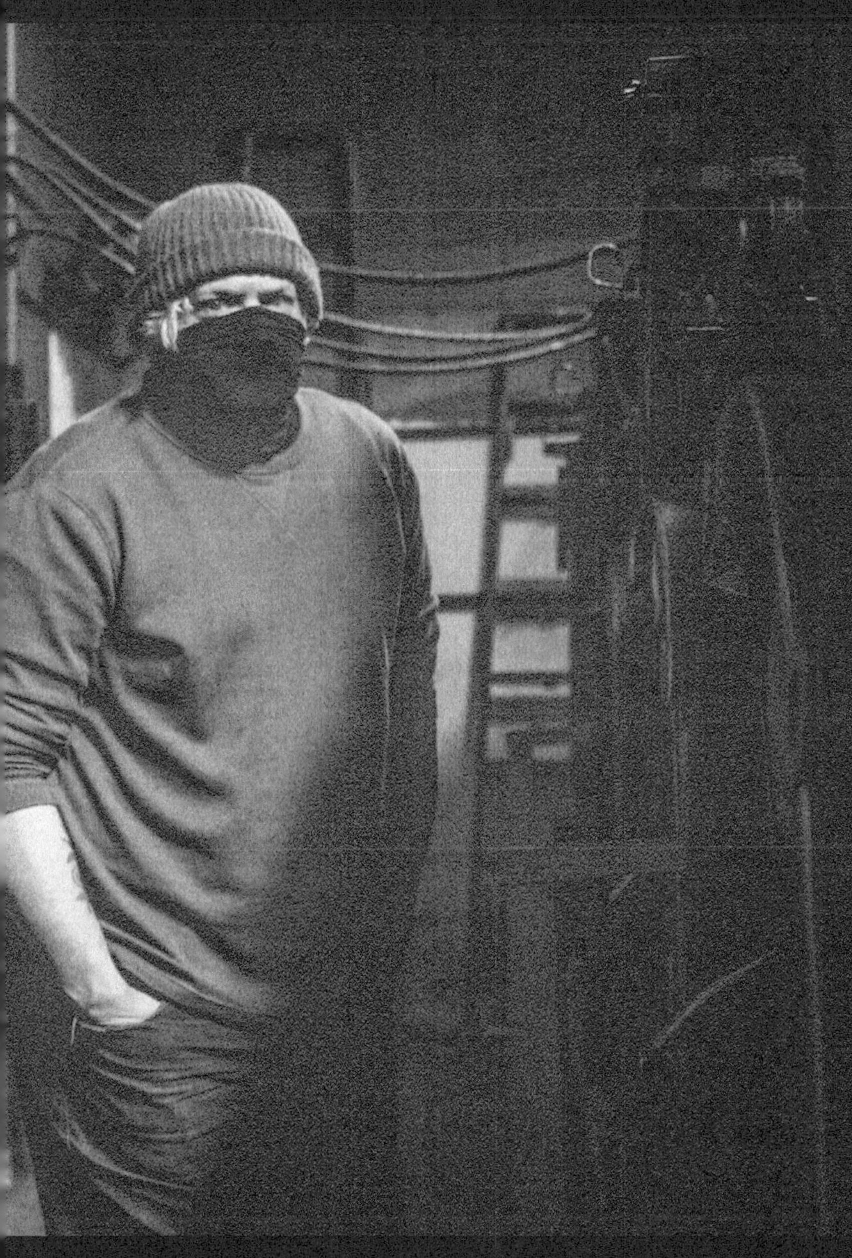

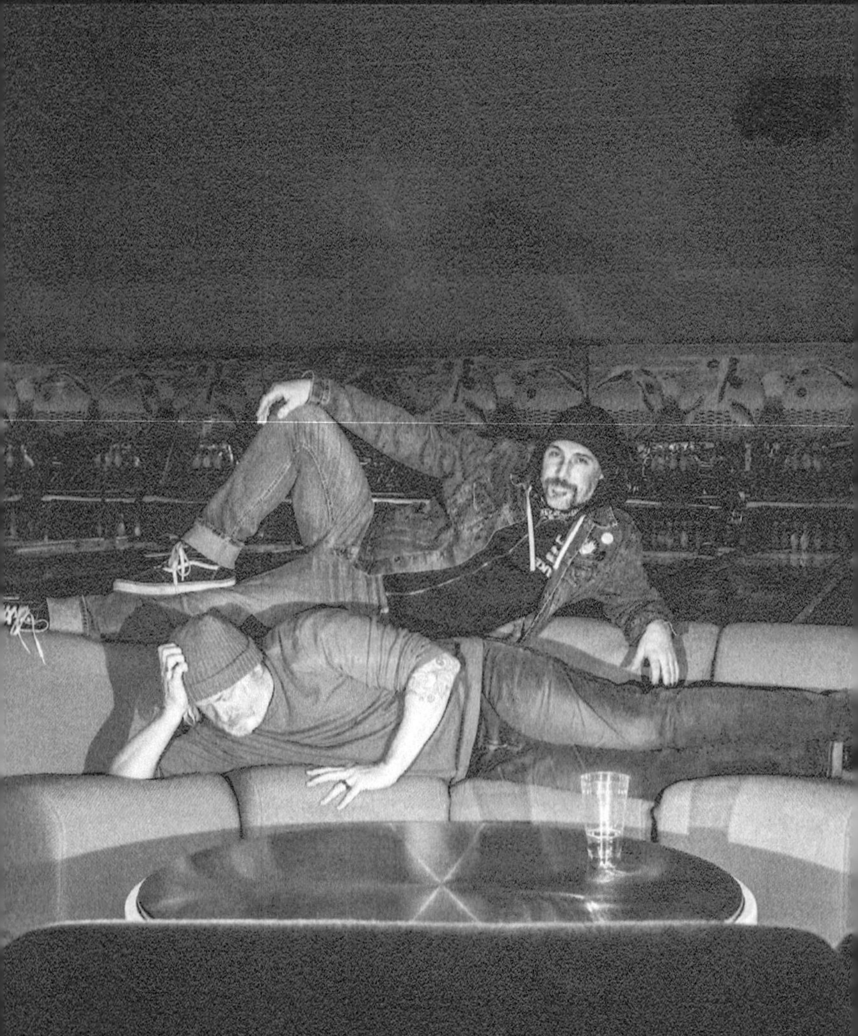

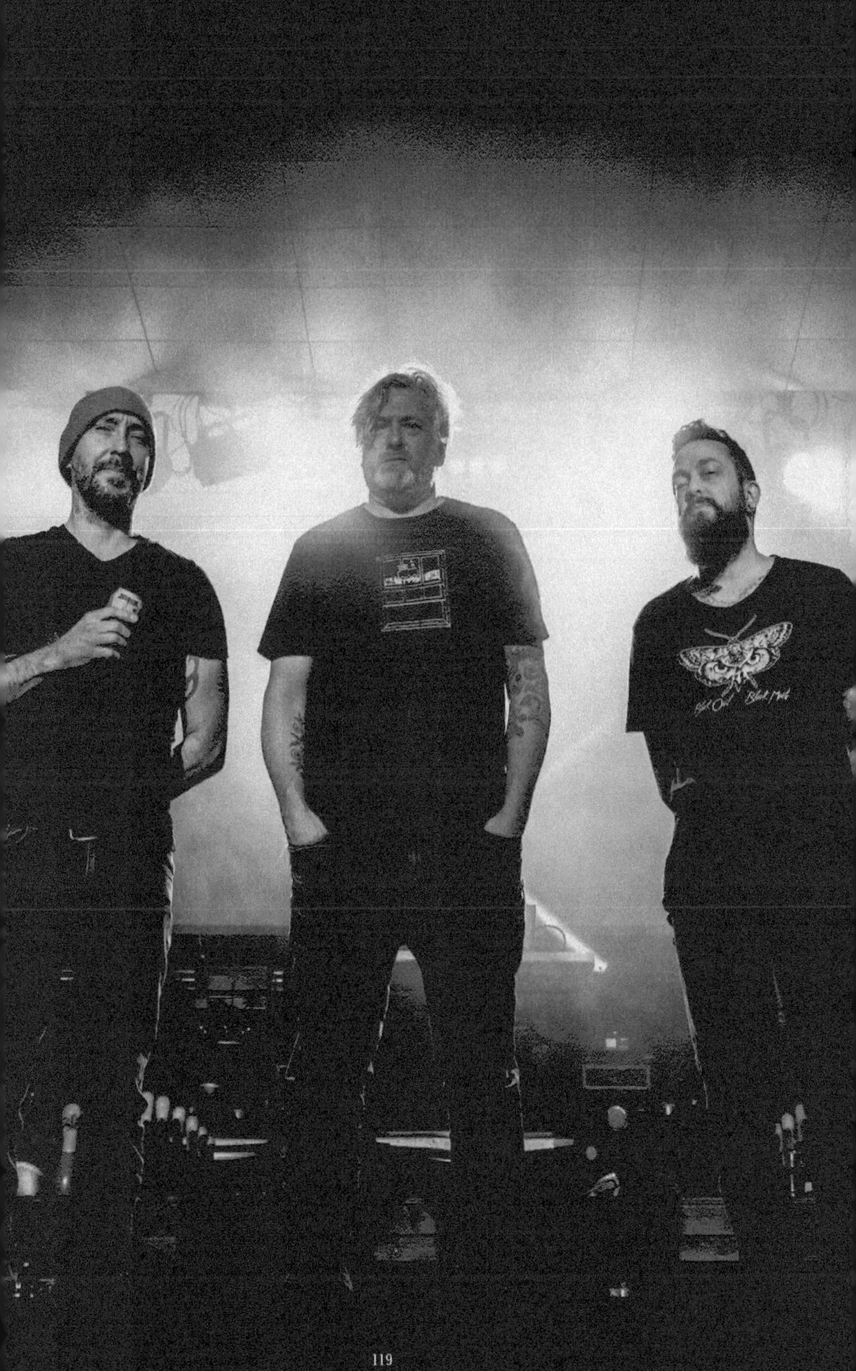

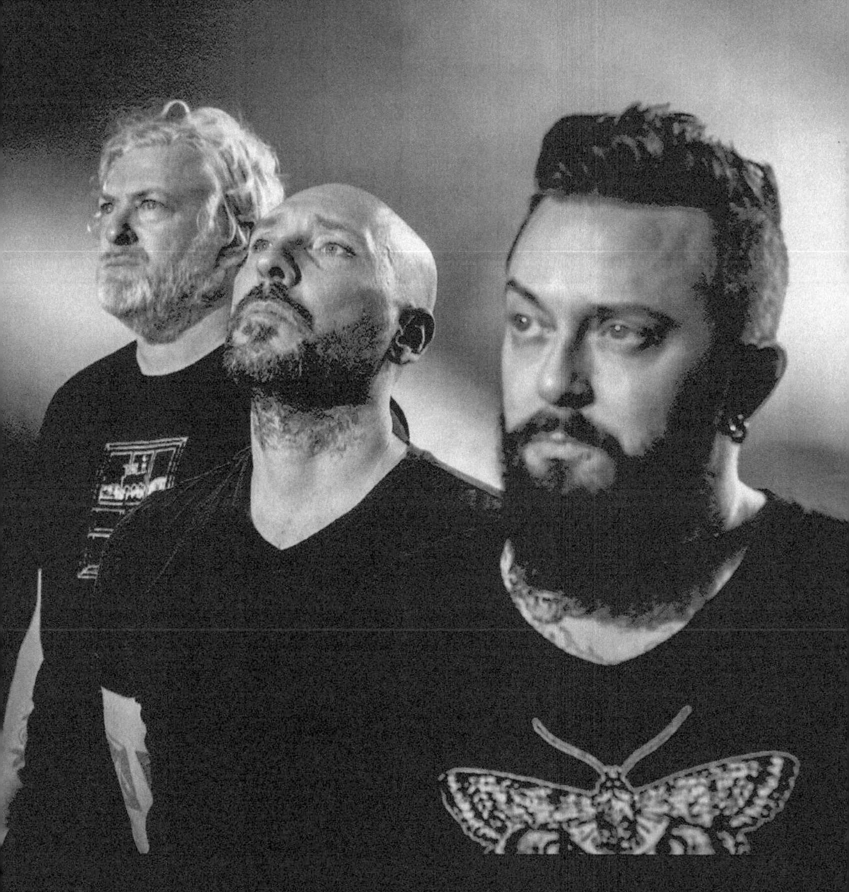

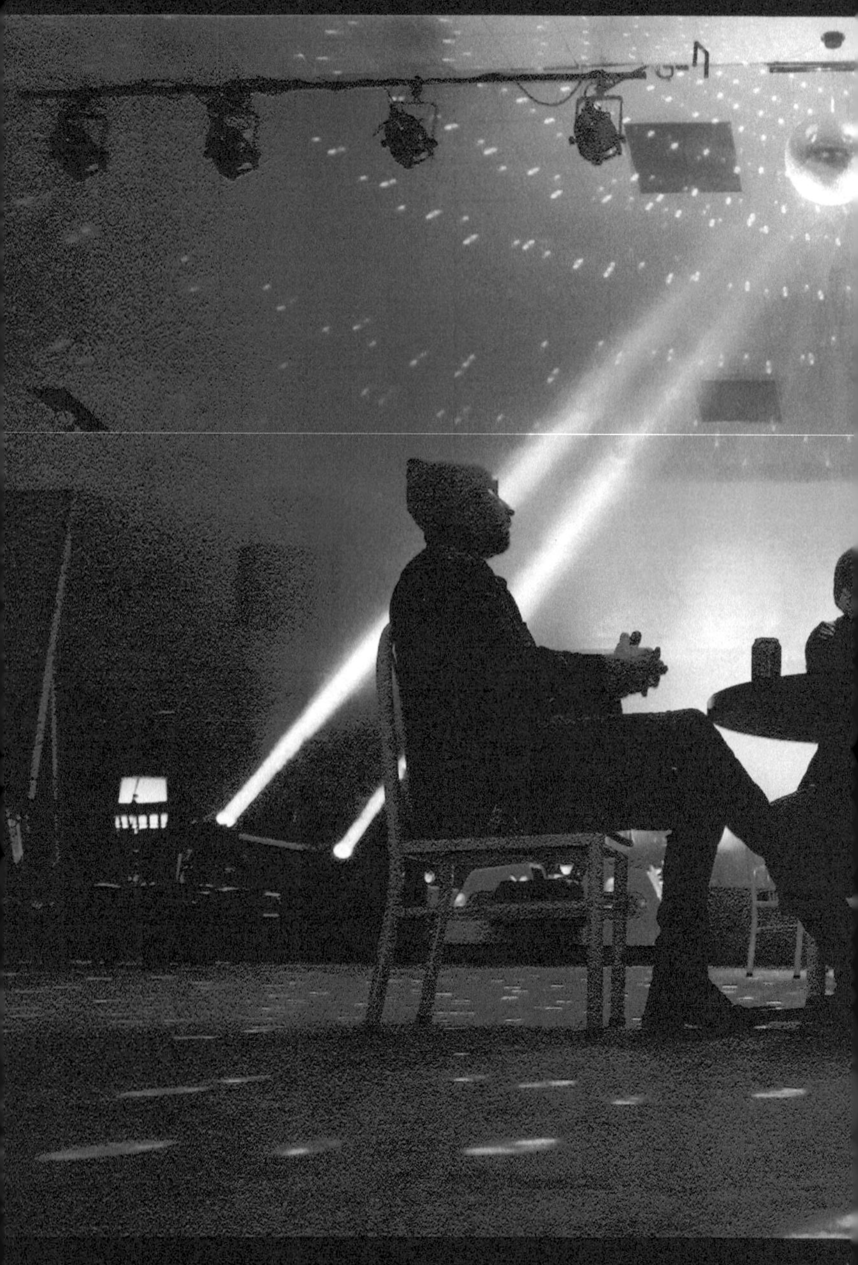

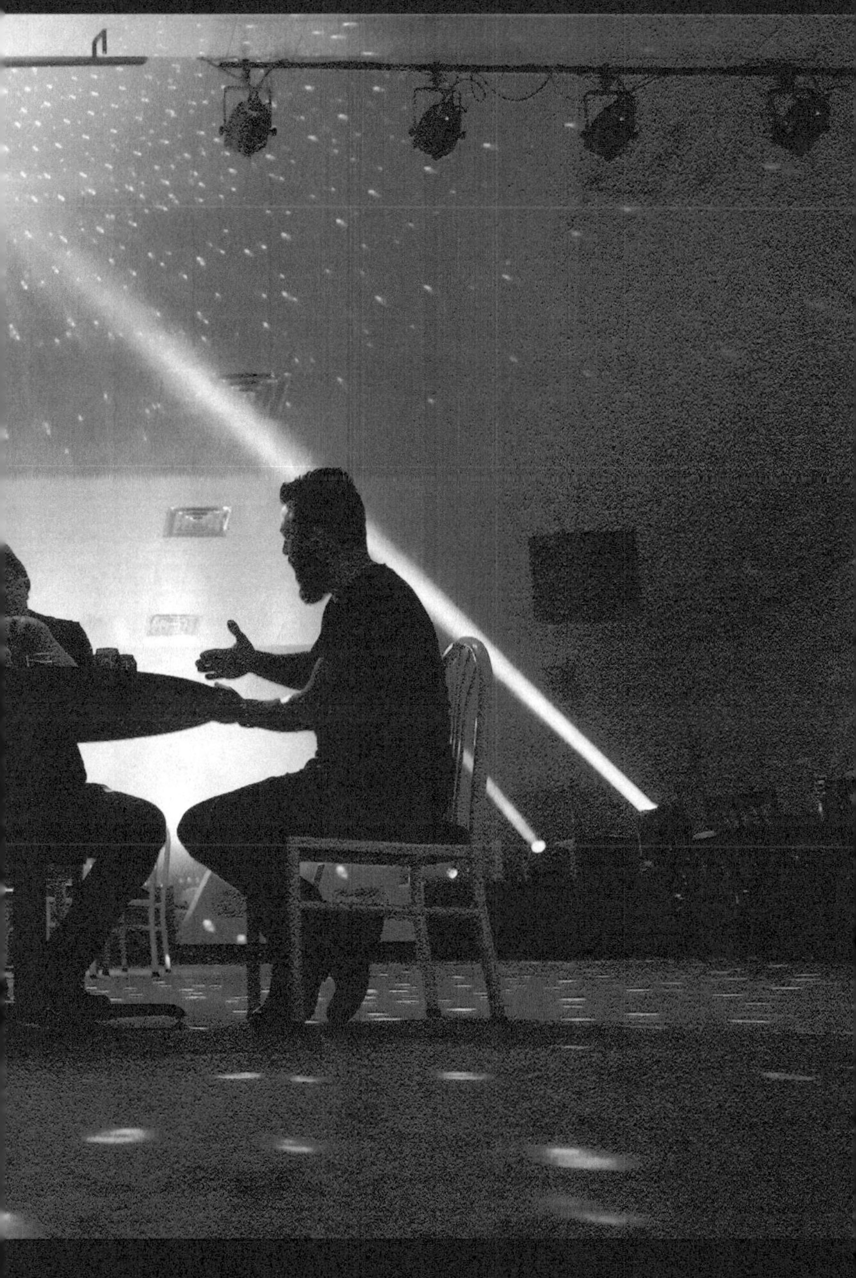

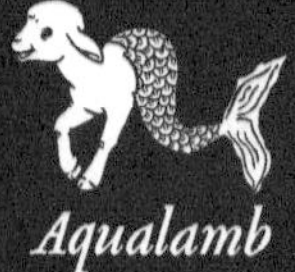
Aqualamb

ALSO Available from Aqualamb Artists

☐ **DESCENDER by Descender** (ALR 001)
6 song debut EP. Available formats: Digipak CD, digital / streaming
90's Influenced post-hardcore. RIYL: Snapcase, Helmet, Quicksand
"Angularly aggressive hardcore that takes an abrasive shape on purpose." – CMJ

☐ **AND SO WE MARCHED by Descender** (ALR 002)
4 song EP. Available formats: Printed book, digital / streaming
90's Influenced post-hardcore. RIYL: Snapcase, Helmet, Quicksand
"...a 21st Century compliant post-hardcore band that was raised on metal and got dosed with a tab of AmRep..."– Jaded Scenster

☐ **TAKING DRUGS TO MAKE MUSIC TO SELL CARS TO by Human Highlight Reel** (ALR 003)
4 song debut EP. Available formats: Vinyl record, printed book, digital / streaming
Instrumental post-rock. RIYL: Maserati, June of 44, Russian Circles
"Aces instrumental post rock. Think Russian Circles or perhaps a more metal Seam..." – Jaded Scenster

☐ **JUDGE by Vagina Panther** (ALR 004)
5 song EP. Available formats: Printed book, digital / streaming
Heavy female-fronted garage rock. RIYL: QOTSA, Cheeseburger, Fu Manchu, Stooges
"Vagina Panther rocks." – Billboard

☐ **BLACK BLACK BLACK by Black Black Black** (ALR 005)
12 song debut LP. Available formats: Vinyl record, printed book, digital / streaming
Melodic death rock. RIYL: Akimbo, Torche, Lungfish, Black Flag
"Brooklyn-by-way-of-Ohio doomsters offer up a big, nasty salute to gas tanks and goat hooves. It all coalesces to form one ravaging feast of melodic death rock that will satiate all your salacious needs, be it Nether-deity worshiping or rock star living." – Broken Beard

☐ **GODMAKER by Godmaker** (ALR 007)
4 song debut LP. Available formats: Vinyl record, printed book, digital / streaming
Doomy sludge metal. RIYL: High on Fire, Red Fang, Mastodon, The Sword
"An example of genuine out of-nowhere brilliance. A patient drawn out campaign of aggression." – Relix

☐ **THE SPACE MERCHANTS by The Space Merchants** (ALR 008)
8 song debut LP. Available formats: Printed book, digital / streaming
Whiskey-soaked space-rock. RIYL: Black Mountain, Dead Meadow, The Besnard Lakes
"A unique brand of lo-fi psych rock... their huge-yet-minimal sound, mixing psych with blues and country style riffs to make something great." – Magnet

☐ **HIRAM-MAXIM by Hiram-Maxim** (ALR 009)
4 song debut LP. Available formats: Vinyl record, printed book, digital / streaming
Noisy experimental doomgaze. RIYL: Swans, Suicide, Pink Floyd, Oxbow
"Builds into an apocalyptic fervor before dissipating into a cloudy haze & ending before you've had your fill." – VICE

☐ **ALTERED STATES OF DEATH AND GRACE by Black Black Black** (ALR 010)
10 song sophomore LP. Available formats: Vinyl record, printed book, digital / streaming
Melodic death rock. RIYL: Akimbo, Torche, Lungfish, Black Flag
"...the kind of good-natured misanthropy of bands like Whores or KEN mode, but the musical gestures beneath the noisy exterior are all forward-charging, Kyuss-worshipping sludge n' roll. It's basically underground metal's version of a radio banger." – BrooklynVegan

☐ **TRESPASSES by Nathaniel Shannon & The Vanishing Twin** (ALR 011)
15 song debut LP. Available formats: Printed book, digital / streaming
Unsettling bedroom recording darkness. RIYL: Lanegan, Badalemnti, Springsteen, Waits
"An unsettling yet captivating collection of songs compiled from a decade of bedroom recordings... Shannon's spoken word-style vocals over haunting and minimalist instrumentals lend a creepy atmosphere to the record." – Decibel

☐ **FERA by Husbandry** (ALR 012)
8 song debut LP. Available formats: Printed book, CD, digital / streaming
Female-fronted math rock meets post-hardcore. RIYL: Mars Volta, Glassjaw, Refused, Deftones
"It's hard to believe that Husbandry is not the biggest band in the world. They're heavy and mathy, chaos wrapped in hard rock and heavy metal." – Nerdist

☐ **MURDEREDMAN by MURDEREDMAN** (ALR 013)
8 song sophomore LP. Available formats: Vinyl record, printed book, digital / streaming
Post-punk inspired noise rock. RIYL: Savages, Bauhaus, Boris, Killing Joke
"A patient and disciplined examination of anxiety and melancholy underpinned with a cathartic tension-and-release structure that borrows from goth, post-metal, and no-wave..." – New Noise Magazine

☐ **IN TENSIONS by Lo-Pan** (ALR 014)
5 song EP. Available formats: Vinyl record, printed book, CD, digital / streaming
Anthemic desert rock. RIYL: Soundgarden, ASG, Torche, Red Fang
"Calling Lo-Pan a stoner band is a disservice to the amalgam of influences the band successfully merges together: the soulful alt rock of the 90s with a thundering doom/sludge sound that's equal parts immediate and timeless." – Nine Circles

☐ **GHOSTS by Hiram-Maxim** (ALR 015)
7 song LP. Available formats: Vinyl record, printed book, digital / streaming
Noisy experimental doomgaze. RIYL: Swans, Suicide, Pink Floyd, Oxbow
"Everything is awash in mesmerizing ambient skree and squalls of atonal feedback. Think an extended, updated version of side 2 of Black Flag's My War." – Hellride Music

☐ **KISS THE DIRT by The Space Merchants** (ALR 016)
10 song sophmore LP. Available formats: Vinyl record, printed book, digital / streaming
Whiskey-soaked space-rock. RIYL: Black Mountain, Dead Meadow, The Besnard Lakes
"[T]he sonic equivalent of having an acid trip in the bathroom between Woodstock and a ZZ Top concert in '69" – New Noise Magazine

☐ **BAD WEEDS NEVER DIE by Husbandry** (ALR 017)
5 song EP. Available formats: Printed book, CD, digital / streaming
Female-fronted math rock meets post-hardcore. RIYL: Mars Volta, Glassjaw, Refused, Deftones
"While retaining their bold go-anywhere style, the EP is a more streamlined and focused effort, signaling a greater maturity and command of recording." – Echoes and Dust

☐ **BY THE GRACE OF BLOOD AND GUTS by Haan** (ALR 018)
8 song LP. Available formats: Printed book, Vinyl, CD, digital / streaming
Noise, Grime, Sludge, Metal, Rock. RIYL: Unsane, Melvins, Swans, Helmet, Clutch
"If Melvins and Unsane had a kid while under the influence of hallucinogens" – Metal Insider

☐ **LUMINOUS VOLUMES by Skryptor** (ALR 019)
7 song LP. Available formats: Vinyl, Printed book, CD, digital / streaming
Noise, Math rock, Prog. RIYL: craw, Dazzling Killmen, Don Cabellero
"Galloping, off-kilter and unabashedly victorious, proggy noise-rock outfit Skryptor's takes hard-rock/psychedelic throwback tropes, flips them on their heads and stretches it all into an adventurous march through endlessly shifting soundscapes."" – Revolver

☐ **DEAD INSIDE by Frayle** (ALR 021)
7 song 7". Alchemy Box: Printed book, Vinyl, CD, digital / streaming
Heavy witch doom. RIYL: Chelsea Wolfe, Portis Head, Sleep, Sunn O)))
"Trades in dark psychedelics and heavy, dripping drums that punctuate the riffing that plays in and around vocalist Gywn Strang's superb voice." – Nine Circles

☐ **SUBTLE by Lo-Pan** (ALR 022)
11 song LP. Available formats: Vinyl, Printed book, CD, digital / streaming
Anthemic desert rock. RIYL: Soundgarden, ASG, Torche, Red Fang
Subtle was produced by James Brown (NIN, Foo Fighters, Ghost) and mastered by Ted Jensen (Mastodon, Deftones, Bad Company, GNR).

☐ **1692** by **Frayle** (ALR 023)

8 song LP. Available formats: Vinyl, Printed book, CD, digital / streaming
Heavy witch doom. RIYL: Chelsea Wolfe, Portishead, Sleep

"Haunting, hypnotic mix of crushing Sleep-style doom and cooing ethereal vocals à la Cocteau Twins' Elizabeth Fraser." – Revolver

☐ **DESTROYER DELIVER** by **Zeb Gould** (ALR 024)

8 song LP. Available formats: Printed book, CD, digital / streaming
Indie-style gloom-folk meets fingerpicking prairie-bliss. RIYL: Neil Young, Gillian Welch, Bill Callahan

"Gould's voice along with his contributors create a sense of warmth throughout their music that makes their melancholic sound comforting and inviting. Destroyer Deliver would be a welcomed addition to any music collection looking to add some mindfulness to their space."– Northern Transimission

☐ **THE THREE MOTHERS** by **Nathaniel Shannon & the Vanishing Twin** (ALR 025)

3 song EP. Available formats: Limited Edition Cassette Box, digital / streaming
THE THREE MOTHERS is a primordial fixation with Dario Argento's trilogy's witches. RIYL: Lanegan, Badalemnti, Springsteen, Tom Waits

"There are very few times that you listen to music and it's something brand new. Something that has it's own identity and style. Nathaniel Shannon's new EP delivers a passionate dark dreamscape of life. His leathery dark vocals are ominous as the music that he creates. Close your eyes and you're suddenly walking down a street with faceless people and distant sound of sirens." – Steve Austin (Today is the Day / Austin Enterprises)

☐ **PRISONER'S CINEMA** by **Burning Tongue** (ALR 026)

11 song LP. Available formats: Vinyl, Printed book, CD, digital / streaming
Crushing nihilism that nod to the shadowy side of hardcore punk. RIYL: Power Trip, Craft, G.I.S.M.

"It's a furious expulsion of nihilistic metallic hardcore, racing and ravaging, clanging and clobbering, seething and slashing." – No Clean Singing

☐ **THE LINE, IT'S WIDTH, AND THE WARDRONE** by **Rebreather** (ALR 028)

8 song LP. Available formats: Vinyl, Printed book, digital / streaming
Doom, Sludge, Metal, Prog. RIYL: Part Chimp, Unsane, Melvins

"...shows that the band are more than mere noise merchants, but an outfit who know how to strike poise and balance, wringing every last drop of catharsis out of the track." – The Sleeping Shaman

☐ **SKIN & SORROW** by **Frayle** (ALR 033)

10 song LP. Available formats: Vinyl, Printed book, CD, digital / streaming
Heavy Witch Ritual Doom Metal. RIYL: Earth, King Woman, Portishead

"[Frayle] create spinetingling devastation doom that curdles the blood and casts dreamy spells, with Gwyn layering gossamer-light My Bloody Valentine-esque vocals over dirgy riffs." – Metal Hammer

☐ **THUNDERHEADS** by **LaMacchia** (ALR 034)

9 song LP. Available formats: Vinyl, Printed book, CD, digital / streaming
Egnimatic layered & moody rock, metal and electronica. RIYL: Liars, Doves, Autolux, Radiohead

"For every rush of adrenaline there's the eventual lull. For each euphoric high there's the comedown to follow. Thunderheads plays like the 3am winding down of a night of excess. Thrills and sensual desires wedded to a shadow of sadness and introspection." – Ghost Cult

---

JOIN THE AQUALAMB RESEARCH CLUB

A record company like Aqualamb releases many albums and books each year. Some of them are by long established artists while others are by people no one has heard of but us. In either case, we'd like to try out some of our upcoming music on you. After all you are the consumer. The final decision is always yours.

So we'd like to know what you think just a little bit earlier. You might say, we'd like to put you into our A&R Department with a little service we call Aqualamb Research Club.

Your role in Aqualamb Research Club is simple. All we want is to hear from you–what you like, what you hate, and why. A year of Aqualamb Research Club will cost you 10 bucks, which just about covers packaging and mailing. In return, you will get a lot of fine music, an Aqualamb T-shirt, and a special Aqualamb Research Club pin plus the chance to influence the course of music. No strings, no gimmicks, no dumb offers or obligations. We just want to tune in to your taste.

EMAIL INFO@AQUALAMB.ORG FOR MORE INFO ON HOW YOU CAN BE A PART OF OUR RESEARCH.

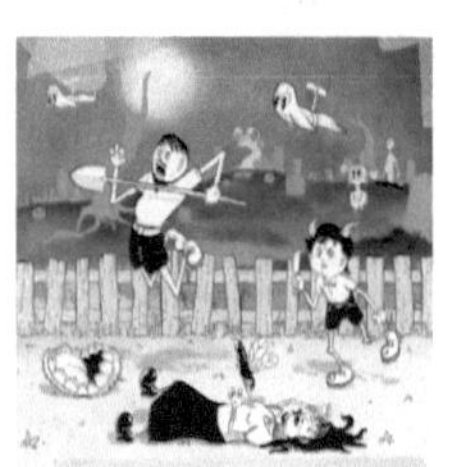

The music for *The Line, It's Width and the War Drone*
can be downloaded via the link below:

aqualamb.org/028

www.ingramcontent.com/pod-product-compliance
Lightning Source LLC
LaVergne TN
LVHW090528110826
845146LV00003B/1017

9798985736533